PRAISE FOR *THE MARTECH*

"In an era of increasingly complex go-to-market strategies, Darrell Alfonso has helped capture some fundamentals that every Marketing Operations and Martech professional needs. What's more, it's an incredible resource for leaders to wrap their minds around the complex (and ever changing) landscape of Marketing Technology."
Mike Rizzo, CEO, MarketingOps.com

"Digital marketing has forever changed how businesses operate. Having personally experienced much of this transformation as it was happening, I can tell you the Martech Stack will continue to expand and evolve as technology, channels, and strategies change. This book is masterfully written and a great blend of current practices, and what's next for Marketing teams."
Nick Bonfiglio, CEO and Founder of Syncari

"Darrell's deep knowledge in how Martech really works in an organization, paired with a thoughtfully researched historical context and visionary foresight into where it's heading makes this essential reading for the seasoned or beginner marketing technologist alike."
Juan Mendoza, Founder and Editor, *The Martech Weekly*

"To be successful in marketing requires an understanding of how marketing technology is used to create the customer experience and to acquire, engage, and retain customers. With this book Darrell Alfonso has made the complex world that is the marketing technology industry accessible and delivers a comprehensive guide to help companies deploy and manage an effective technology strategy. This is a must-read for anyone in marketing or the C-Suite."
Anita Brearton, Founder and CEO, CabinetM

"Bible to all marketers. Martech is an integral part and lies at the center of any Marketing organization and all Marketing leaders must have a basic grasp and understanding of Martech. This book is the

bible to understanding bringing the right Martech and the right people to orchestrate the strategy and the tools together."
Jessica Kao, Director, F5 Networks

"The explosion of Martech in the last decade is a phenomenon that is defining potential and future of marketing as a profession and a discipline. If you're in any way interested in Martech, and what it means for your career in marketing, this book is a must-read."
Joel Harrison, Co-founder and Editor-in-Chief, B2B Marketing & Propolis

"Today, every business is a digital business where consumers are in control of the buying experience. Yet, while marketing technology is foundational to building your brand and growing your business digitally, most senior leaders don't understand 'Martech.' Which is why this book is essential, as it enlightens us on how we leverage the power of marketing technology now and in the future."
Cassidy Shield, Chief Growth Officer, Refine Labs

"*The Martech Handbook* is a must for every modern marketer. With the acceleration of digital transformation in the world there has never been a more important time for marketers to build their knowledge and capabilities in Martech. This book provides a deep dive on the core principles of marketing technology success including stack design, gaining stakeholder Martech buy-in and developing robust marketing operations governance."
Carlos Doughty, Founder and CEO, Learning Experience Alliance

"Marketing is now thoroughly a technology-powered discipline. To thrive in today's environment, marketing organizations need to develop strong, mature marketing operations and Martech capabilities. You couldn't ask for a better guide to achieving than Darrell Alfonso, a pioneering Martech industry leader and marketing ops pro. *The Martech Handbook* is a treasure map to world-class marketing in an age of digital transformation and beyond."
Scott Brinker, Editor, chiefmartec.com

"This is chalked full of real-world advice to unlock the value of Martech. A must-read for any marketer thinking about or in the throes of using tech and tools to run marketing like a business."
Scott Vaughan, Go-to-Market and Martech Strategist

The Martech Handbook

Build a Technology Stack to Attract and Retain Customers

Darrell Alfonso

KoganPage

First published in Great Britain and the United States in 2022 by Kogan Page Limited

2nd Floor, 45 Gee Street
London
EC1V 3RS
United Kingdom

8 W 38th Street, Suite 902
New York, NY 10018
USA

4737/23 Ansari Road
Daryaganj
New Delhi 110002
India

www.koganpage.com

Kogan Page books are printed on paper from sustainable forests.

ISBNs

Hardback   978 1 3986 0646 3
Paperback   978 1 3986 0644 9
Ebook   978 1 3986 0645 6

British Library Cataloguing-in-Publication Data

A CIP record for this book is available from the British Library.

Library of Congress Cataloging-in-Publication Data

2022938415

Typeset by Integra Software Services, Pondicherry
Print production managed by Jellyfish
Printed and bound by CPI Group (UK) Ltd, Croydon CR0 4YY

This book is dedicated to Janet, and my family, Etchell, Angelita, Edmund, Phillip and Andrew.

CONTENTS

ABOUT THE AUTHOR

Darrell Alfonso is an award-winning marketer and Martech professional. He was named one of the top Martech Marketers to Follow in 2020, won the Fearless Marketer award in 2018, is a 2X Marketo Champion, and is a certified Salesforce Administrator. He has consulted for several Fortune 500 companies including General Electric and Abbott Laboratories and currently leads marketing operations at Amazon Web Services where he helps empower hundreds of marketers to build world-class customer experiences. He is a frequent speaker at Martech events, and regularly posts thought leadership content on LinkedIn and Twitter.

01

Introduction—The Rise of Marketing Technology

I have a fabulous, fruitful, and exciting career because of Martech. I would argue that it is the same for top marketing professionals everywhere—they've been able to create amazing marketing value because of marketing technology. I was first introduced to Martech in my first job working for a tech startup in 2010. We were marketing and selling a software-as-a-service (SaaS) that helped businesses engage customers via new digital channels. I didn't think of it as Martech at the time. In my mind, we were helping businesses grow through the use of software, technology, and platforms.

But I became fascinated by how interwoven marketing and technology had become. As with many who work in the startup life, I talked to literally hundreds of customers, from small businesses to enterprises. I quickly noticed that the more I learned about marketing, the more I saw how technology could be used to make it better. And it became increasingly clear that in today's digital economy, marketing and technology could no longer be thought of separately. Today, it doesn't make sense to think about marketing in a silo and to isolate it from all the digital channels and touchpoints that customers experience when they engage with brands. Doing so would be incredibly abstract, and be void of all the practical things required to make marketing a reality. Conversely, to only think about technology is also a trap, because you'll miss out on all the strategic and creative value that humans bring to creating meaningful customer experiences.

Technology without creativity is like using an inefficient energy device—we'd input ten units of energy and get two units as the output. But combining the two ideas together—the creative with digital; and the strategic with automation—creates incredible value, and that's what I really love about marketing technology.

I have worked in marketing and Martech roles for several years, initially at startups and mid-size companies before moving to my current role at one of the world's leading organizations. In each role I have leveraged marketing technology to enhance customer experiences and drive tangible business results. When it comes to smaller companies, Martech helps the business acquire new customers faster. It allows teams to be agile, and to continually test new strategies to optimize for the best possible outcomes. For mid-size companies, Martech can help solidify a company's position by connecting sales, marketing, and customer success to support continual revenue growth. Martech reveals which programs are the most effective, and how to constantly surprise and delight your customers. For large enterprises, Martech can help thousands of employees create value for customers in every region of the world, in a scalable, compliant, effective way.

Not surprisingly, the growth of Martech has exploded across all industries and geographies. I often think back to a marketing technology conference in 2016 when Scott Brinker—founder of Martech blog *ChiefMartec*—debuted the Martech 5000. The Martech 5000 is a graphic that shows 5,000 logos from different marketing technology companies. Attendees came from far and wide to be the first to see the new graphic. You could feel the excitement in the room as marketers struggled to be the first to snap a picture of the graphic with their smartphone and post it online for their colleagues back home to see.

The Martech 5000 graphic (which is now the Martech 8000 as of 2021) is a testament to the growth and power of marketing technology and the role it plays for both businesses and customers alike. But how did the Martech scene come about? Where did Martech come from, and how did it get so popular?

Let's First Define Martech

Simply put, Martech is a blend of the words marketing and technology, and refers to any digital platform or tool that helps marketers achieve their objectives. You'll find that I use "Martech" and "marketing technology" interchangeably. Commonly, the objectives of Martech are to attract, engage, convert, and delight customers, and there are specific Martech platforms that can support all of those objectives.

When a business has multiple Martech tools and platforms that integrate and work together, this congregation of technology is called a "Martech stack," sometimes referred to as "tech stack."

Let's provide a practical example: a marketing team could use an advertising platform to promote content on different channels. The leads generated from those advertisements would be stored in a marketing automation platform (MAP) and customer relationship management (CRM) platform. The marketing automation platform would be used to deploy lead nurture campaigns to engage and convert prospects into customers. A customer loyalty platform would automatically identify ways to enable and reward your best customers. The Martech stack in this specific example, refers to the advertising tool, marketing automation platform, customer relationship management platform, and customer loyalty platform.

But Isn't All Technology Martech?

In a LinkedIn poll of 654 marketers, 41 percent of respondents said that Martech is any tool that marketing owns or manages. (All the LinkedIn polls referred to in this book were conducted in December 2021 with different numbers of participants. All contained an equal mix of Martech specialists, managers, and leaders.)

It may be tempting to categorize any tool the marketing team uses to get their work done as Martech. For instance, the average marketer will use Microsoft Outlook and Slack to communicate with their teams, PowerPoint and Adobe Photoshop to create presentations, and Microsoft Excel or Google Sheets to perform analysis. In addition, the marketer's company will have a number of software programs running in the background that the marketer uses but may not be conscious of, such as antivirus programs, single sign on (SSO) and virtual private network (VPN) management, and payroll services. But the key distinction is that any professionals across multiple disciplines can also use these tools to get their work done. Therefore, there is little value in categorizing those tools as marketing technology.

Most of the Martech that we cover in this book will be technology that is specifically developed to serve marketers, meaning that marketers are the primary intended user of the platforms. However, since Martech is inexorably linked with various sides of the business, such as sales, operations, finance, and customer success, we will go in-depth into the technologies that marketers can't live without, but whose primary purpose wasn't necessarily to serve marketing initiatives.

As previously mentioned, there is multitude of use cases for Martech, and thousands of tools currently in the marketplace. To get a firm understanding of how we got here in the first place, we'll first take a look at Martech's history.

Martech Through the Ages

If you think about Martech as technology that helps marketers achieve their objectives more effectively and efficiently, Martech has really been around a long time. Especially if you consider analog technology, or non-digital tools. The printing press enabled marketers to circulate their messages across millions of magazines to reach consumers all around the world. The video camera helped brands get their spokespeople in front of the masses through home television sets. And in terms of marketing measurement, I would argue that the calculator was probably the first piece of truly helpful marketing technology; enabling marketers to record, tabulate, and keep better track of their marketing efforts.

Continuing this line of thinking, we'll look at marketing technology through the decades.

In the 1970s, before most consumers were using the internet on a daily basis, the only way to reach customers was through print and traditional advertising. Computers were introduced, and marketers used them to organize audience lists. Imagine trying to figure out how many mothers with multiple children in a specific state and in a specific socio-economic demographic, and cross-referencing that with their mailing address. In addition, computers enabled marketing to record, tally, and calculate the effectiveness of these efforts to analyze and report back to the business.

In the 1980s, we saw a large migration to digital, though not the digital that we know and love today. The Martech of this period centered around campaign managers and sales automation, and we began to glimpse the introduction of applications and programs to manage telemarketing and loyalty programs. The 1980s also included the emergence of spreadsheets (predecessors to Microsoft Excel), and the statistical analysis of marketing industry began to rapidly improve.

In the 1990s, we saw consumers finally begin to use the internet. The use of email for both personal use and business use started to resemble what it does today, and we saw the rise of e-commerce and general online marketing. The marketing technology of the period, however—with the emergence of email marketing platforms and web analytics, SEO and basic attribution platforms—was pretty unexciting compared to what it is today.

The decade of the 2000s was when Martech really hit its stride, with much of the key platforms being founded during this period. The large players of marketing automation, which is one of the largest and most defining categories of Martech, were founded in the 2000s, with Marketo, Pardot, Hubspot, and Eloqua all coming onto the scene and growing at a rapid pace. Alongside these major platforms emerged social media and content marketing platforms, video marketing tools, customer data platforms (CDPs), digital asset management (DAM), and predictive analytics—all of which we will cover later in this book.

The decade of the 2010s saw the advancement of all the aforementioned categories, with the introduction of complete journey orchestration platforms, and much of the advanced artificial intelligence (AI)-based strategies and tactics, such as machine-generated content, AI workflows, and personalization.

Now in the 2020s, we are beginning to see the consolidation of many of the Martech tools and platforms. Large categories such as marketing automation, data management, and customer experience are encompassing much of the Martech stack. Point-solutions (tools that serve a single, primary purpose or function) are sprouting in many categories, to later be consolidated into one of the large platforms.

Now that we've looked back over the decades, let's deep dive into the reasons for Martech's growth in popularity.

Key Reason for the Rise of Martech: The Rise of Consumer Digital Consumption

I was a voracious reader growing up (and still am) and couldn't get enough of books, magazines, newspapers—you name it. This was my preferred way to consume information. Even though I still love to read books, it's hard to ignore the fact that the way we consume information has changed, even in the short time frame of my childhood to adulthood.

The most immediate sources of news are now social media platforms. We get the latest happenings from a tweet, Instagram post, or Facebook story. It might be from a journalist, our favorite celebrity, or just about anyone for that matter. When it comes to short stories, podcasts are now the most popular medium—with episodes streamed on Apple Podcasts, Spotify, and Amazon Music. As for good-old books, 90 percent of the time I consume them on an eReader or as an audiobook. Looking back, it's fair to say that the consumption of information has certainly been disrupted.

It wasn't long ago that our great grandparents only received their information through the daily paper or on the few radio or television channels available at the time. This made marketing relatively simple: create an advertisement and broadcast or print it on the only channels that consumers were paying attention to. But alas, it is a very different picture today. Reaching consumers is an omnichannel effort.

Omnichannel refers to communicating to customers on all possible mediums and touchpoints, from billboards and in-store displays, to web, social media, apps, and beyond. Because consumer consumption of information is now primarily digital, it takes a coordinated effort with the use of a multitude of technology to create, deploy, and measure marketing.

Take, for example, the effort required to launch a social media advertisement. A marketer could use an online SAAS design tool such as Canva to create the ad images and copy. Next, they would log in to Facebook's ad manager to identify a target audience determine the ad spend. After the campaign has been deployed, the marketer can log into Google Analytics to compare their average traffic and conversions with the new visits they get through their social media campaign. This basic example of a marketing campaign process demonstrates how much Martech is involved in engaging customers on digital platforms.

In short, the ways to reach consumers have been barreling towards a digital-first reality since the invention of the computer screen, and marketing has been forced to evolve. Today, instead of creating billboards and national tv ads, marketers are developing creative for all digital channels, following consumers wherever they go across the web. With Martech being almost fully consumed by digital, this contributes to the overall adoption, use, and rise of marketing technology.

Key Reason for the Rise of Martech: The Digital Transformation of Business

It's fun to imagine a time when office workers punched physical time cards to mark the beginning of their shift. And how long ago was it that everyone dreaded the correction memo from the movie *Office Space* landing on everyone's desk when a mistake was made?

While these antiquated activities seem like they are from a distant era, it was only ten to fifteen years ago when most businesses operated this way. What may seem like an obvious use case for digital, activities like this are actually very challenging to make "digital first." This is especially true for large, enterprise companies with several thousands of employees. When businesses migrate their analog activities to digital, it is called "digital transformation," and it's been a popular trend the past few years.

But it's not an easy task. Take the mega brands of Ford and GE, for example, who invested over $1 trillion in digital transformation initiatives, only to fail and revert back to traditional business operations (Kitani, 2019).

Thought daunting, most businesses soon discover that the value of transitioning to digital far outweighs the cost of implementation. Teams can get comprehensive, timely reporting on all aspects of their business, creating the agility to make swift pivots or course corrections when the need arises. In addition, digital operations make it easy to review historic performance, combine data sources, and perform complex analysis and modeling to help determine their future decisions and investments.

Here are just a few statistics on the state of business digital transformation (Finances Online, 2021):

- The global digital transformation market is projected to grow from $469.8 billion in 2020 to $1,009.8 billion by 2025, at a compound annual growth rate (CAGR) of 16.5 percent during this period (Research&Markets, 2020).

- Digitally transformed organizations are projected to contribute to more than half of the global gross domestic product (GDP) by 2023, accounting for $53.3 trillion (IDC, 2020).

- 65 percent of the world's GDP is predicted to be digitized by 2022 (IMF, 2020).

- 70 percent of organizations have a digital transformation strategy or are working on one (PTC, 2019).

- Industrial enterprises are seen to have benefited the most from digital transformations (PTC, 2019).

- 55 percent of startups have already adopted a digital business strategy (IDC, 2018).

- 38 percent of traditional businesses have adopted a digital business strategy (IDC, 2018).
- 89 percent of enterprises are planning to adopt or have already adopted a digital business strategy (IDC, 2018).
- Top digital business strategy adopters include services (95 percent), financial services (93 percent), and healthcare (92 percent) (IDC, 2018).
- 39 percent of executives expect to benefit from their digital transformation initiatives in three to five years (Fortinet, 2018).
- 21 percent of North American and European enterprises say their digital transformation is complete (Forrester, 2018).

How Martech Works

Before we dive too deep into Martech and all that it can do, it's important to get a high level of understanding of how Martech typically works in an organization. First, marketers and their adjacent colleagues purchase marketing technology from software vendors, the contract of which is typically in the form of a software-as-a-service (SaaS) subscription model, where businesses pay a monthly or annual subscription fee to access services over the internet. These various marketing technology platforms can either be used in unison or separately, and there is variety in terms of overall connectivity, strategy, and usage of each platform. This depends highly on the Martech strategy, talent, and budget.

We see the savvy marketing teams integrating Martech platforms, which means configuring the tech stack in a way that data flows readily between multiple systems. Ideally, this configuration is a bidirectional sync, which means that records are continually updated to be the same in multiple systems, which promotes data quality. These well-architected Martech stacks enable teams to leapfrog others who must spend time manually cleaning and processing data. Integrating Martech platforms also reduces technical debt, which is the accumulation of tasks and effort required to fix issues that arise when leveraging multiple technologies in a way that doesn't support long term success.

Not all teams enjoy this luxury. Many companies have varied levels of interconnectivity in their tech stack, and some platforms remain completely siloed. This creates work in the form of manually exporting and importing data, cleaning spreadsheets of data, and reconciling differences between multiple databases.

Regardless of how well the Martech stack is interconnected, the business will have a Martech team of people (formalized or not formalized) who own and operate the different components of the tech stack. We'll get into the roles and responsibilities in Chapter 8 of this book, but for now keep in mind that each Martech platform requires a sponsor, an owner, and an operator—and these can be separate members of the team or the same person.

Martech as an Industry

The terms I would use to describe the Martech industry are: exciting, staggering, fast-growing, and a bit overwhelming. In 2019, Clickz estimated the value of Martech in the North American and UK markets as $65.9 billion, and globally at $121 billion (Collins, 2019). In terms of growth, what once was an industry of 150 Martech tools in 2011, shot up to over 8,000 Martech tools in 2021. That is an explosion of Martech. You can actually see all 8,000 listed on the Chief Martec website (https://chiefmartec.com/).

As shown in Figure 1.1, each component of the Martech industry evolves to drive it forward:

Competition: While tremendously exciting for marketers around the world, and especially those selling Martech services, this can be quite overwhelming when deciding which Martech tools to use and how. The industry is also incredibly competitive—many categories of tools have dozens of options with almost identical functionality and pricing. Let's take an example from the Martech 5000 database; a public, free database that lists out the majority of Martech tools available. In the category "content and experience" and sub-category of "email marketing" there are 223 companies to choose from. Of

FIGURE 1.1 Martech Industry Drivers

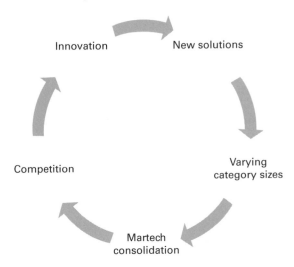

the ones I've had the pleasure of working with, I know that Mailchimp, Constant Contact, Campaign Monitor, and Emma all have fairly comparable monthly and annual plans to pick from. So, which do you use?

Varying category sizes: One other distinguishing characteristic of the Martech industry is that some of the categories play a much bigger role than others, and often take up more of the Martech budget. Examples of these categories are email marketing, marketing automation and data management. When it comes to smaller categories such as video marketing and influencer marketing tools, marketing teams will pay significantly less. To give a real example of the differences, "marketing automation" as a category is large and are typically over six figures a year in cost. Since this is a larger, more mature category, it has since been dominated by large software companies. Some of the main players in this space are Marketo, owned by Adobe, Pardot by Salesforce, Eloqua by Oracle, and Silverpop by IBM.

Emergence of marketing clouds: At the time of writing, the large software vendors such as Adobe, Salesforce, and Oracle are working on building "marketing clouds." Marketing clouds are a suite of Martech platforms that serve a variety of marketing needs and are owned by the same company. While you don't necessarily log onto the same portal to access all of these services, the added benefit is better inter-connectivity between the services and a single vendor contract. Only time will reveal if there will eventually be one dominant marketing cloud to "rule them all."

Always new solutions: An exciting feature of the Martech land-scape is that there are new categories and platforms emerging all the time, as digital continues to disrupt marketing and the business marketplace at large. Many of these new platforms only have a handful of features and benefits they offer, but are relatively inex-pensive and quick to implement, providing immediate value to the marketing team. There are even many "point solutions"—a service that only provides one primary business value. For example, Sigster, acquired by Terminus, helps marketers put ads in employee signa-tures. UTM.io is another example, and its sole purpose is to help marketers organize UTM parameters. While these point solutions help marketers move quickly and save time, it has the added conse-quence of creating massive Martech stacks that are difficult to manage and govern.

Potential Dangers When Working with Martech

While Martech may seem like all the buzz, and it can indeed help you and your marketing team increase your effectiveness and scale expo-nentially, there are some common problems that often arise. These pitfalls can plague marketing teams of all sizes, regardless of the experience of the team:

- buying too many tools;
- shiny object syndrome;
- underutilizing/shelfware;
- being feature-driven versus strategy-driven.

1. Buying Too Many Tools

In a LinkedIn poll of over 1,000 marketers, 51 percent of respondents said that the biggest challenge in Martech today was too many tools and too little strategy (Figure 1.2).

FIGURE 1.2 LinkedIn Poll Results

What is the biggest challenge in Martech today?

You can see how people vote. **Learn more**

High on tools, low on strategy ✓	51%
Lack of skilled talent	17%
Lack of integrated data	30%
Missing functionality	2%

1,142 votes • Poll closed • **Remove vote**

The lure of marketing technology, especially today, is that there is a tool for everything. Most problems that marketers are facing have a corresponding point solution out there in the marketplace. And with the plethora of tools to choose from, compounded by technology becoming more advanced and affordable, it can be tempting to string together any and all tools to help get our work done. The problem with this strategy is that it can get quickly out of hand, lead to an incoherent strategy, and worse, a discontinuous customer experience because of all the different platforms you are using to engage and measure their behavior.

2. Shiny Object Syndrome

One thing we know about marketers (myself included) is that we love new things. We love exciting new platforms that promise new ways of engaging customers and making our lives easier. Whether it be a new tool to advertise on the latest social media platform, or an integration tool to connect all of our projects and work together in a seamless way, the lure of purchasing something that can change our work life is a very human feeling. The challenge becomes that these shiny new objects may not fit in with our overall Martech or marketing strategy, and may not be what is best for engaging customers long-term. But we can't help but be tempted...

3. Underutilizing Technology (Shelfware)

When marketing teams subscribe to too many tools, what often happens is that many of these tools go unused. An example could be a testing tool that the team purchased last year doesn't conduct any tests, or a data management tool that is hardly utilized because data initiatives are deprioritized. These tools have been satirically referred to as "shelfware" because they sit on a hypothetical shelf, going unused by the marketing team that expected to realize value from it. The cause of this is twofold: first, it is the aforementioned issues of purchasing too many tools and grabbing the latest shiny new object. Second, it is the lack of Martech talent—people who know how to technically and strategically get the most value out of each tool and set them up for success—and overall cohesive Martech strategy to deliver return on investment (ROI) for each platform.

4. Being Feature-Driven versus Strategy-Driven

Another common temptation is to use all the features that Martech has to offer. Some of the large marketing automation platforms boast hundreds of marketing features that teams can leverage to drive impact with their work. The problem? Not all of these features are useful, and in some specific business cases, very few are. But the motivation of getting a return on expensive software, and using everything a platform has to offer, is very tempting. Unfortunately, marketers can get too caught up in trying to use the features, and forget what the goal of using those features was in the first place. The answer to this tragedy? To set your marketing objectives first, and then select the features and tools that will help you achieve them.

I painfully remember an example of how being feature-driven versus strategy-driven can negatively impact business. I remember being so excited about being the lead administrator for a marketing automation platform for a medium-sized business. The first thing I did? Figure out all the features and functionality that my team wasn't using, and started to put them into place. After several months I had tried out the different bells and whistles with little success, and was confronted by a very tough question by my leader: "What did we accomplish these past few months?" he asked intently, curious since I seemed so busy. My heart fell flat. The truth was, while I was consumed with busy work, trying to implement all the features that the platform had to provide, I realized that I never stopped and asked the key questions: What is most important? What are we trying to achieve? And which features and tech would it take to get us there? Needless to say, that conversation didn't go very well, and it is still a strong reminder of why we need to always think about our goals, objectives and strategy before we think about trying out new tools.

Martech as a Profession

More and more people are working in Martech, as the number of technologies—and their respective use cases and impacts—continue to grow. The reason? Martech doesn't operate itself. It would be nice if you could subscribe to a social media advertising/data analytics tool, and simply wait for more leads and amazing business insights to pop out. Unfortunately, however, that is the furthest possible thing from the truth. Operating and getting value out of Martech takes two non-negotiable things: talent and time.

From a talent perspective, many of those who work in Martech are digital marketers. Some have transitioned over from a generalist marketing role, such as a marketing manager, planner, or specialist, having had a special proclivity for tools and tech. Another great many will have fallen into managing Martech, or just because of the nature of their jobs needed to leverage the variety of technology at the company's disposal. While many Martech platforms are intuitive and can be learned by the average digital marketer, there are some software that require a bit more technical expertise and experience. The common platforms that require more technical expertise than your average digital marketer are marketing automation, data management, and integration platforms. Because of this need, some marketers can make a career out of learning and specializing in specific enterprise platforms, and many do so by going into consulting.

The time component of managing Martech also needs to be taken into consideration, because the projects and time value often have a long horizon. On the far end of the spectrum, enterprise Martech tools that will be used by hundreds of employees can sometimes take six months to implement, and longer to train and gain adoption. In addition, the results from Martech can take a while to come to fruition. Take, for example, the launch of a new content marketing platform. It will take months before content gets enough traffic, converts leads, and generates revenue before an ROI is realized.

One thing that is certain—the demand for Martech professionals is growing exponentially, and, at the time of writing, a search on LinkedIn for Martech professional roles reveals that there are currently over 100,000 open roles available.

What's the Difference between Martech, Marketing Operations, and Marketing Automation?

The concepts and terms of Martech, marketing operations, and marketing automation are often confused, and in the worst case, used interchangeably. While there is definitely overlap between the three terms, it is important to distinguish each. Martech refers to the technology (tools, software, and platforms) that helps marketers do their jobs. Marketing operations is the function that operates the tools, processes, and data to help marketers do their jobs. Marketing automation is a category of Martech that focuses on programmatically executing many of the activities a marketing team typically does. The reason these three terms are typically confused is because Martech is typically owned and operated by the marketing operations team/ function. Marketing automation is one of the largest components of the Martech stack, and marketing operations professionals will typically spend a disproportionate amount of their time in managing that specific platform. For example, at the enterprise level, marketing automation platforms have millions of records in their databases and deploy thousands of campaigns per year. These large platforms require dedicated professionals to administrate and govern the platform. These professionals are all Martech professionals working in marketing operations, but their entire job will be dedicated to marketing automation. You can see how this can be confusing. While many of the success principles that we will cover in-depth in this book apply to all three concepts, it is important to recognize the nuances of each in order to derive the most possible value.

Martech Can Be Very Technical

One thing people don't think about is just how technical Martech can be, from a role standpoint and an implementation standpoint. The core of Martech is rooted in systems, applications, and digital marketing, which has always required the more tech-savvy marketers to operate. First, realize that the customer experience of Martech is some sort of web experience, either on a desktop, mobile device, or app. This in itself requires some level of web development expertise, and Martech managers often need to know the basics of Hypertext Markup Language (HTML), Cascading Style Sheets (CSS), and JavaScript. You'll see marketers often customize assets such as emails and landing pages with these languages, though they may not be the ones to create the assets initially. The next point is that the Martech platforms themselves can be quite robust, and require platform-specific knowledge to operate. For example, most customer relationship management systems (CRMs), marketing automation platforms (MAPs), and customer data platforms (CDPs) are large database platforms with several layers of features and tools that require months of training to master. These tools often offer multiple tiers of certification as a means of training and demonstrating expertise. The implementation and operation of Martech can be so technical, that an entire industry of Martech consulting has been created, with some of the largest consultancies like Deloitte and

Accenture having teams dedicated to marketing technology, and it can be quite lucrative for independent of boutique firms as well. There are some firms that specifically dedicate themselves to the consulting of one platform, examples of these are Salesforce and Marketo. The technical expertise and operation that this industry requires is also evidenced by the rise of the low-code/no-code movement, as popularized by Scott Brinker. The low-code/no-code movement is the creation of platforms that allow non-developers to create applications and platforms for themselves. Many marketers have taken full advantage of this by using these low-code/no-code platforms to build their marketing technology and solutions. This is a very exciting time to work in Martech!

How This Book Is Organized

This chapter, as you have seen, introduces us to Martech and its storied past, as well as some of the reasons why we've seen such explosive growth of this category.

In Chapter 2 we'll cover the business need for Martech, and key business goals marketers can accelerate and achieve by utilizing marketing technology to its full potential.

In Chapter 3 we'll talk about the major categories of Martech, and the purpose and similarities of all of the tools within each category, as well as some of the major players in each space.

Chapter 4 will talk about what a Martech stack is, its makeup, and how different organizations of all sizes use Martech stacks to achieve their objectives.

Chapter 5 will be an important chapter, where we will talk about the framework for designing an effective Martech stack. This includes how to audit your current technology stacks, assessing your future needs, and how to select the best Martech platforms for your situation and business.

In Chapter 6 we talk about the core business systems and platforms every marketing team needs. While there are over 8,000 Martech platforms on the market today, and the permutations and combinations are infinite, there are some basic/mainstay technologies that marketers require, otherwise they will not be able to do their jobs effectively.

Chapter 7 helps a marketing team identify new tools and platforms to add to their Martech stack, no matter what maturity stage they are in.

In Chapter 8 we'll delve into the principles of how to ensure you are getting the most out of your Martech stack and future Martech tools.

Chapter 9 is a deep dive into the tactics you need to drive adoption and effectiveness from all of your marketing tools.

In Chapter 10 we talk about people. Getting buy-in is paramount when rolling out new tools and rolling out big changes. Nothing happens without working with and influencing people.

In Chapter 11—our last chapter—we'll talk about the things you need to continue to grow and get more effectiveness out of your marketing technology, regardless of the technical advances of this rapidly growing industry.

02

The Business Need for Martech

Why Do Businesses Need Martech?

Now that we have an idea of what Martech is and what contributed to its rise in popularity, this chapter will take a deeper look at the business value Martech can bring to an organization. Businesses can use Martech to better engage with, create value for, manage, report on, and optimize for, the digital customer. Let's break those down.

Digital Engagement of the Customer

Consumers today are digital. They work and play across websites, apps, social media, and more. Marketing technology is the toolbox we use to create great experiences across all of these channels and mediums. Let's take email for example. Consumers are reading from their inbox daily, opening messages from family, their employer, and commercial messages from brands. A marketing team would use email marketing software (under the promotional category of Martech) to actually create and deploy the email experience to the customers' inbox. However, this goes way beyond email: customers engage with brands in many different places, such as company websites, social media feeds, audio platforms, streaming services, and video-sharing platforms. All of these channels require different marketing technology to produce, manage, and deliver an overall ROI for the brand.

Another of my favorite examples is using marketing technology to host a virtual conference. In-person live events are great opportunities for brands to give customers a place to learn, network with others, and overall have a memorable experience. The challenge is that live events are expensive to host and can be inaccessible to many customers for various reasons. In addition, the recent safety precautions brought about by the COVID-19 pandemic make today's live events even more complex and risky. A fantastic alternative to this is a virtual conference. Using Martech, brands can emulate much of the benefits and live experiences the attendees would receive at an in-person event, but from the comfort of their own home or office. This also completely eliminates travel costs, venue fees, and saves a ton of preparation time for both the host and the guests. A great example of this was when the software company OpenExo decided to transform their ExO World Summit event into a virtual conference for 2,800 attendees and 130 speakers (OpenExo, 2019). Using an all-in-one virtual conference platform, OpenExo hosted large keynotes, breakout sessions with smaller groups, speaker meetings, and even one-to-one networking opportunities—all online and over the internet.

Martech Helps Create Value for Customers

Did you know that marketing can create significant value for customers? Done right, marketing helps customers discover products and services that can help them solve their most pressing problems. You can then think of Martech as creating the road for marketing to transport marketing messages and delightful experiences to customers. Martech helps the marketing team transfer the important ideas and concepts that can help customers improve their lives.

Martech can also help customers learn, take for example, my first marketing role many years ago. I was working for company that offered mobile and social media services to small business in the form of an online platform service. One of the key challenges was adoption: customers were having difficultly learning and using the product. This occurred at key times during the customer journey, which was affecting sales; the free trial wasn't going well and customers were quitting the service when they couldn't figure out how to use it. My team and I used a combination of email automation as well as webinar marketing to identify key moments when prospects and customers needed help the most, and automatically triggered educational emails and how-to webinar invitations. After just a few weeks, the customer engagement and churn metrics improved significantly. This is an example of Martech creating value for the customer (in the form of education at critical points) as well as the business.

Collect and Analyze Marketing Metrics to Optimize

I ran a poll on LinkedIn in August 2021 of 654 middle- and senior-level marketers from companies of all sizes (Figure 2.1). Forty-nine percent reported that the most important business need that Martech served was "to use data to improve marketing." Compared to the other survey options ("create engaging experiences," "automate business processes," and "the better management of marketing"), this survey indicates that data is extremely important to marketers and the role it plays in overall marketing success for the business.

With marketing today being almost entirely digital, it's paramount to report on and analyze campaign results with the goal of optimizing your entire program. For example, if you were running a paid social media ad on Facebook, you would be able to see the total impressions,

FIGURE 2.1 Important Values Martech Creates for Business

What is the most important value Martech creates for business?

You can see how people vote. **Learn more**

Create engaging experiences	**15%**
Use data to improve marketing ✓	**49%**
Automate business processes	**25%**
Better management of marketing	**11%**

653 votes • Poll closed • **Remove vote**

clicks, conversions, and leads generated from the campaign. This is achieved through Facebook's ad platform (which is in the promotional category of Martech) but can be improved upon by leveraging a BI or analytics tool to compare Facebook data to other channels. This can also demonstrate how the campaign impacted sales overall.

Reporting and analytics are also critical to reviewing the efficiency of your customer funnel. For example, a common marketing funnel model begins with "awareness," through to "interest," "consideration," "purchase," and "advocacy." "Awareness" makes up the large top of the funnel portion, and "purchase" and "advocacy" make up the narrow bottom portion of the funnel. Martech tools in the analytics category of Martech help us understand the engagement and conversion rates at each stage of the funnel, and can shine a light on problem areas. This is where Martech can help assist with our marketing optimization efforts (Figure 2.2).

Capture: Martech platforms used for analytics help capture important data points from different channels and mediums, and aggregate salient data into one place for analysis.

Management: In addition to compiling data, Martech tools can be used to synthesize, standardize, and normalize data so it can used in an actionable and comprehensible way.

Visual analysis: Many Martech platforms offer a method of visualizing and displaying important marketing and customer datapoints,

FIGURE 2.2 The Components of Martech Optimization

so that initiatives can easily be compared against each other. In this way, Martech enables marketers to pull insights from the data, separating the "signal from the noise."

Predictions: Increasingly, there are new Martech platforms powered by artificial intelligence (AI) and machine learning (ML) capabilities that can automatically sift through terabytes of data quickly and use algorithms to predict customer behavior. Today, there are AI/ML-powered Martech platforms that can identify marketing programs with the highest probability of success, and automatically deploy changes to marketing initiatives in real-time, skipping the need for human intervention entirely.

Managing Marketing to Improve the Customer Experience

The cornerstone of great marketing (and great business practice) is a great customer experience. Harvard Business Review defines customer experience as "encompassing every aspect of a company's offering—the quality of customer care, advertising, packaging, product and service features, ease of use and reliability" (Schwager and Meyer, 2007). You can also frame the customer experience in terms of the five senses: touch, taste, smell, sight, and sound. How does the product feel in the hands of the customer? How does the restaurant appetizer taste? How does the shampoo and conditioner smell? What music plays in the store? What does the customer see when they visit your website? All of these experiences combine to create a feeling and mental reference when customers think of your brand.

Improving the experience directly: Martech can be used to improve the customer experience directly. This easily lends itself to a digital example, where Martech can be leveraged to personalize a website or email experience to the needs and preferences of each customer. Brands can use cookies to track a consumers internet activity, such as which web sites they like to frequent, and then use real-time personalization tools to offer up specific visuals, copy, and offers that would be most appealing.

Understanding customers to improve future experience and business decisions: Analytics Martech platforms help us collect and analyze data, which helps us understand how customers are experiencing our brand. We can take those learnings and apply them to our business decision-making, helping us improve the customer experience in the future. Take the website for example: if reporting reveals that many visitors are quickly bouncing from our site, it's a strong indicator that the experience is not relevant, and/or the campaigns driving traffic to our site may be confusing or misleading. This is a signal for us to spend time improving that area.

Martech Automates Repetitive Processes

Let's revisit the LinkedIn poll of 654 marketers, where I asked the question: "What is the most valuable business need Martech serves?" In second place, 25 percent of the respondents said that the most valuable business need that Martech serves is to "automate business processes."

While marketing is generally considered a creative endeavor, like most jobs, it isn't void of tedious and repetitive tasks. Examples of this include managing spreadsheets of leads, identifying which leads attended an event, and sending the same type of email campaign over and over again. Marketing automation, one of the core categories of Martech, automates all of these tasks and more, and frees up marketers to spend more time on strategic and creative initiatives. Many Martech platforms go far beyond automating simple tasks, and can almost automate most of the customer journey. Add to that the fact that Martech platforms can be used together in a Martech stack, there isn't much on the digital front that you cannot automate. Here is a real example: Let's say a prospect watches a video on your website. Based on the video type and time viewed, a video marketing platform could trigger an email in your marketing automation platform, with a link to view other similar pages on your site. When the visitor views those pages, a chatbot could pop up, asking the prospect if they would like to meet with a salesperson to see a demo in real-time. All of this happens without the need for human intervention. Amazing! While there will always be a need for a human touch in sales and marketing, Martech can remove the burden of time-consuming, repetitive tasks.

Martech Helps Achieve Alignment

A key challenge that plagues sales and marketing teams is alignment. Sales always wants more leads, and more qualified leads, and often blames marketing for any shortage. This is caused by lack of transparency and shared goals, as well as lack of visibility into the different priorities that each team is working on.

Implementing a solid Martech strategy can help the go-to-market team (sales, marketing, and customer success) achieve alignment. Martech can help with efficiency, transparency, and communication. In terms of efficiency, let's take a look at lead scoring and lead routing.

Lead scoring is a feature of a marketing automation platform, and ranks leads based on their demographic and behavioral characteristics to gauge sales readiness. Lead routing is sending the right lead to the right sales team at the right time. Both of these greatly improve efficiency by having sales spend their time working with leads that are most likely to purchase, rather than wasting time with leads that are just "window shopping."

Transparency is another great alignment opportunity. Martech reporting and attribution platforms enable marketers to share marketing's performance across the entire organization. This helps stakeholders understand marketing's business impact, and also helps surface any collaboration opportunities. Customer data platforms also help drive alignment, by uniting disparate data sources so that sales and marketing have one view of the customer. Martech also improves communication, whether to help teams collaborate on projects or highlighting which leads are sales-ready. For example, marketing project management tools can help marketers from different teams and regions all work of the same, collaborative project platform. Another example of communicating important data is sales intelligence and predictive analytics, which arms sales with the information they need to have timely and impactful conversations with prospects and customers.

Technology is Advancing Every Part of Our Lives

Take look at our daily lives—there's evidence everywhere of how technology is improving our lifestyle. Our smartphones give us access to almost limitless information, our Wi-Fi-enabled home appliances keep us warm and comfortable, and wireless technology allows us to make financial transactions easily and securely. Social media platforms connect us to our loved ones around the world, and remote work technology empowers distributed teams to collaborate and deliver results quickly.

In the same way that our lives are made better through technology, marketing is improved by Martech. Consider the multitude of customer touchpoints, from awareness all the way to advocacy. Each of these touchpoints can be improved through technology. Customers searching online can discover similar or adjacent products to meet their needs, they can learn about solutions through interactive online experiences, and they can use pricing calculators and shopping comparison tools to help them make the right decision. Even advocacy can be greatly improved by using Martech to help customers refer their friends or write a delighted review.

Martech Helps You Know and Understand Your Customer

One of the key benefits of Martech is a deeper understanding of who customers are and what they want. Many categories of Martech tools—from advertising to email, and video marketing to data management—all have built-in reporting features. Though the primary use case of these platforms may not be analysis, the enormous amount of customer engagement data we receive from these touchpoints gives us a better view of our customer. By combining, structuring, and reviewing all of these touchpoints, we take a big step toward understanding our customers more and making better decisions on how to serve them.

Martech Helps Drive Marketing ROI

One thing that we'll cover in detail is how Martech can help marketers increase and measure marketing ROI for the business. An ongoing challenge for marketers proving their value is connecting their activities to revenue and overall business impact. Martech helps drive marketing ROI in a few ways:

1 Targeting the right customer with the right message at the right time.

2 Personalizing marketing campaigns to improve customer experience and conversion rates.

3 Continually driving customer value throughout the customer journey.

4 Connecting marketing activities to revenue to improve decision-making.

1. Targeting the Right Customer with the Right Message at the Right Time

Martech tools enable marketers to better segment their audience. Segmenting an audience refers to selecting a subset of a population that you believe would best benefit from your offer; this subset is known as your target audience. Advertising platforms help identify these subsets, other engagement platforms such as email and marketing automation enable marketers to slice and dice a database into perfect target audience lists for campaigns. Once a well-defined target audience is selected, the probability of marketing success is greatly improved.

2. Personalizing Marketing Campaigns to Improve Customer Experience and Conversion Rates

Though a target audience will share many characteristics, each customer will have their own individual preferences. Personalizing a marketing campaign means tailoring the creative, copy, and offer to the individual, based on data we know about the customer from previous interactions. When a potential customer feels that a message is customized to their particular preferences, they are more likely to buy.

3. Continually Driving Value Throughout the Customer Journey

Why stop marketing when a prospect becomes a customer? There are Martech tools that support loyalty programs and other customer marketing initiatives, such as identifying when customers need help using your product or service, as well as rewarding loyal customers and advocates with gifts and rewards. When customers feel that they are getting great service, can overcome challenges when working with your business, and are appreciated, they are more likely to buy again and refer their friends.

4. Connecting Marketing Activities to Revenue to Improve Decision-Making

Martech tools such as marketing automation, tag management, data management and marketing attribution help take all the campaigns that marketing puts forth and attaches them to dollars that they bring in. This is incredibly valuable, since it helps marketers understand which of their programs is working and which are underperforming. One important point is that marketing ROI and attribution is not about proving which team or individual gets credit for sales and revenue, but about helping the business as a whole to understand where they should invest future budget and resources.

Marketing Management

Martech enables marketers to get their work done more effectively and efficiently. There are Martech and project management platforms that assist large and small teams in collaboration and execution. Imagine all of the steps and tasks required to launch a large user conference? How about announcing that latest version of a product? In the past, marketers used paper and pens to track campaign budgets, reports, and customer feedback. Today, all of that is digital; it's online and stored in the cloud. Martech can be used to manage those different assets in a streamlined way. Many advertising platforms for example, offer functionality to track your campaign budget, create enticing digital ads, and continually tweak marketing investments to optimize a program over time.

I personally remember being so impressed when working with a client who had implemented a project management platform that had been custom-designed to support marketing teams and their campaigns. Here's how it worked: First, a campaign request would be entered into the platform by a campaign owner. This campaign request had all the necessary fields and allowed for creative assets to be uploaded, so that the executional arm of the team would have everything they needed. Next, other members were added to the request, including an operations team and content approvers. The operations team could then create the email campaign, and the project management platform integrated directly with the email platform, allowing both the campaign owner and content approver to review the email content without having to use multiple systems. Upon final approval, the operations team was notified to perform technical quality assurance (QA), and then deploy the campaign. This platform reduced an incredible amount of back and forth between multiple parties, helping to streamline campaign operations.

Martech and Globalization

One of the great things about Martech is that it helps with the globalization of marketing, enabling companies to execute consistent marketing efforts across different regions, as well as help marketing teams in different countries take advantage of technology to connect with their customers. Most of marketing technology is available online, as a software-as-a-service (SAAS). This means that marketing teams can log into Martech from anywhere in the world, only needing an internet connection. This is a quite important point, because there are under-resourced and under-funded teams in various parts of the world that can operate like big companies with the use of Martech. In addition, there are Martech tools that enable marketing information to be translated and localized for different regions. Many marketing teams source a global marketing campaign or message from headquarters in one country, and need to disseminate the same message to their customers across every continent. The use of Martech to customize marketing per region helps marketing be inclusive and accessible. Martech also helps large teams that span across several regions to work together in a collaborative way. In the case of many robust Martech platforms like marketing automation platforms and customer relationship management platforms, teams can each have custom accounts with unique features and data sets so they can do their marketing independently, while still leveraging the benefits of the resources of the greater company.

In my personal experience, I've set up more than a dozen teams on one Martech platform. Each team had access to marketing templates that they could customize for their own purposes and in the language of their choice. The databases were also separated, which made it easy to understand the market for each region and run reports and analysis separately, while still being able to use one primary system. The separation of a database into specific section is called "database partitioning." While these teams could operate their marketing program independently, they were all governed by one central team. This central team ensured compliance and brand guidelines across the core marketing functions but allowed flexibility for each group to tailor assets when it made more sense for their customers.

Key Signs You Need to Invest in a Martech Strategy

Now that we've seen the key business needs that Martech fulfills, let's review some indicators that your company may need to invest more into your Martech strategy.

Your Business is Lagging Behind the Pace of Digital Change

Many companies today are still behind the ball when it comes to digital operations, particularly those from the manufacturing and industrials sectors where they've relied heavily on antiquated methods of production, delivery, and communication. This is rapidly changing, especially with the pandemic accelerating the need to produce and consume from far distances. The term "digital transformation" is now a buzzword of the modern economy. Digital transformation can be defined as the "rethinking of how an organization uses technology, people, and processes in pursuit of new business models and new revenue streams, driven by changes in customer expectations around products and services. For many enterprises that build traditional goods, this means building digital products, such as mobile applications or an ecommerce platform." (Salesforce.com) In short, many companies don't possess the necessary talent and resources to support today's digital marketing efforts.

How can you tell if that is the case for your company? Begin by reflecting on a few questions:

- Would you define the people in your organization as tech-savvy?
- Are the people in your organization using the latest software and programs? Are they primarily working online and in the cloud?
- Are the people in your organization working collaboratively using online services in real time and in a remote environment?

If you answered "no" to any of these questions, it's a good sign that the work that you do can be greatly enhanced with Martech.

Marketing Efforts are Repetitive and Manual

One of the painful memories I have is being responsible for a monthly, comprehensive marketing report that was presented to leadership. It took me almost two full days to compile the data and create the report, and on top of that, it was littered with errors when I was done with it. All of that changed when I learned how to leverage a customer relationship management system (CRM) paired with a data analysis tool. After just a few weeks of properly setting up the data model and creating the reporting frameworks, can you guess how long it took me to create the monthly report? Actually, it didn't take me any time at all. The report was now fully automated and in real time. That is the power of automating manual efforts. In addition to saving a lot of time, because the reports were being pulled by a machine/computer and not tabulated by hand, all of the data was correct 100 percent of the time. So, not only was Martech faster at creating the report—it was better.

Is your marketing too time-consuming and painful to implement? Here are some questions that can identify if Martech can help:

- Is your marketing primarily performing data-entry type tasks?
- Are your team filling out forms all day?
- Is much of their time spent on the phone or in meetings where they are asking other teams or vendors to implement campaigns for them?

Answering "yes" to any of these questions is a tell-tale sign that your team is not self-serving and could be leveraging technology to perform their work instead of going through an intermediary. There is an entire category of marketing technology known an "marketing automation." Its goal is to eliminate the tedious, repetitive tasks that slow marketing teams down.

Marketing Cannot be Done Without Relying on Technical Resources

Once upon a time, marketing teams had to rely on engineers and IT resources to launch most of their digital initiatives. For example, pulling a subsegment of customers from the company database required the help of an IT or systems administrator. Creating email campaigns with images required contracting or hiring a front-end developer who specializes in HTML and CSS. Actual delivery of said email would require additional engineering resources to deploy from the company email server. The situation is very different today: marketing team's do not have an excuse to not be able to plan, create, execute and report on a simple digital marketing campaign. In the aforementioned example, a marketing automation platform integrated with a customer relationship management platform enables marketers to query customer lists in real time, as well as use self-service editors to build the email experience. All a marketer needs are basic design principles and some copywriting experience—no technical knowledge needed.

I personally remember my first marketing job. Every email and landing page would go through a single process:

1 Copywriting and mockup.

2 Submission to graphic designer.

3 First review.

4 Upon approval, submission to publisher (someone who converts design to HTML).

5 Testing and QA.

6 Review and final approval.

This was the process every single time! Today, there are Martech tools that allow marketers to create their own emails and landing pages with WISIWIG (what-you-see-is-what-you-get) editors, with the result being vibrant, creative assets that are responsive across all devices. That outdated six-step process is no longer necessary.

Your Data is in Chaos

One of the big issues plaguing businesses today is the lack of data insights and data-driven decisions, and this applies especially to the marketing team. The underlying challenge is a lack of a data-first culture, which means that decisions are made more on opinion and gut feeling, which can be subjective, biased, and incredibly off-course. But that challenge is perpetuated by lack of access and visibility into the data. Not being able to see what is working and what is not working is a surefire recipe for failure. Imagine trying to stay under the speed limit without your odometer, or trying to bake a cake without knowing the temperature of your oven: "Well it feels about 350 degrees, I think we should leave it in there for 10 more minutes...."

That analogy illustrates how hard it would be do effective marketing without using data to inform your decisions. The messaging strategy, campaign ideas, channels, and offers would all be guesswork. It's important to take all the data points that campaigns generate, analyze them over time, and ultimately improve what is not working.

Take stock of your data situation and ask these questions: Do you have access to the data you need? Is the data complete and reliable? Do you receive the data from a single source or from multiple sources? Is the data you receive in an actionable format or does it require significant cleaning before it can be used? If you answered yes to any of these questions, it's a good sign that you need Martech to set your data strategy straight. Martech reporting and data management platforms help build a unified view of your customer, and connects data together from different sources to report, visualize, analyze, and action upon.

You're Part of a Fast-Growing Organization

When you're part of a fast-growing business, the constant growth customers, employees, and resources becomes unwieldy. Marketing in particular finds themselves having to run campaigns in more regions, and against more customers. The volume of data and number of technologies a team uses skyrockets, and teams can quickly find themselves overwhelmed. Martech can alleviate these growing pains by aligning tools and resources, identifying efficiencies, and helping develop a holistic and integrated marketing approach across all customer touchpoints and platforms. For large organizations, this type of alignment can be almost impossible to achieve by working in spreadsheets or over email. Martech workflow and project management tools are an example of technology designed to help growing organizations sustain growth in a practical way.

The Varying Levels of Martech's Importance in Business

A growing concern among marketers is the lack emphasis put on Martech and its importance to the marketing function and to the business overall. On one hand, some of this is variable depending on industry and company size. For example, startups and tech companies have long seen the importance of technology to improve all areas of the business, and recognize how technology can help marketing teams scale and grow quickly. Conversely, companies in the industrial sector, or businesses that have been slow to embrace digital transformation, have been resistant to technology of all kinds, and this is not different in the marketing department.

Regardless, it has been a broad concern that many companies do not invest in Martech at the appropriate level, and even more so in the areas of talent and training. In other words, many marketing teams feel there could be tremendous business value in buying additional Martech solutions and to invest in the people to operate them, but they are having a hard time getting budget approved. There are two primary reasons for this: First, marketers struggle to quantify the ROI Martech brings, of which we'll talk in-depth later on in this book. Second, many executives don't grasp the need for technical talent and training for marketers. Historically, leaders only needed to hire development resources to create product. Today, technical resources are needed in almost every area of the organization.

Though the value of Martech is quickly becoming more recognized as the industry grows, many sectors still have a long way to go when it comes to the proper investment in Martech.

Important Martech Trends to Keep in Mind

Before we get into the "what" and "how" of Martech stack design and management, it is important to keep in mind a few key things that are continually influencing the Martech landscape and how businesses use it.

The Empowerment of Non-Technical Talent

One of the key things that continues to drive Martech innovation is the desire to enable marketers to move faster and get their job done more independently. Whenever there is a task that marketers rely on other departments for—such as engineering and development tasks or financial analysis or project management—third parties will continue to create tools to serve those needs. We've seen this already in the development of the content management system (CMS) to help marketers build and manage websites, as well as powerful data analysis tools that help marketers visualize and analyze data.

Consolidation

The companies and solutions in the Martech ecosystem continue to compete for marketing budgets and strive to meet more of a company's marketing needs. To meet this demand, we'll continue to the pattern of mergers and acquisitions among technology companies. If Vendor A serves one marketer need, and Vendor B serves another, the two vendors may see a winning strategy in joining forces and having both services in one platform, or at least together on one bill. Several major Martech acquisitions have occurred over the last decade:

- Adobe acquired Marketo in 2018;
- Salesforce acquired ExactTarget in 2013;
- Salesforce acquired Tableau in 2019;
- Discover.org acquired Zoominfo in 2019;
- Demandbase acquired Engagio in 2020;
- Twilio acquired Segment in 2020.

As Martech continues to rapidly change, we will be sure to see more consolidation in the future.

Data Integration and Synchronization

One of the pervasive problems that we continue to see in Martech is data existing in multiple systems and data being different in multiple platforms. We therefore continue to see entire categories of products being created to address that need, from the customer data platform

(CDP) to the integration platform as a service (iPaaS) that we'll cover in-depth in later chapters. The inherent challenge that arises from having multiple tools in a tech stack causes increasing data quality and accessibility issues, and this will continue to be true for the foreseeable future.

Marketers Creating In-House Solutions

A subject that we will touch on in later chapters is the concept of "proprietary Martech," which involves businesses building their own Martech tools with their own resources. This could be as simple as a technically proficient marketer who is using low-code platforms to build a custom integration between two systems, or as complex as having product managers and a team of developers create a robust, in-house marketing system. The key drivers for this trend are advances in digital technology allow many non-engineers to create technical solutions increasingly on their own and budget constraints and resources sometimes lean businesses toward making their own solutions versus buying. In addition to data privacy and security, especially at the enterprise company level, force businesses to create their own solutions rather than trust third parties to keep their customers' data safe.

Summary

- Businesses need Martech to help engage and create value for customers.
- Martech also helps marketers collect and analyze marketing metrics to optimizing marketing programs and improve decision-making.
- Martech also helps teams achieve alignment, and automate tedious, repetitive tasks to create more efficiency.

- Organizations that are falling behind the times can use Martech to bring their marketing into the new age.

- There are important trends worth watching in Martech, including the empowerment of non-technical talent, the consolidation of marketing tools, and the need for unified data.

03

Key Categories of Martech

Introduction

In this chapter, we are going to talk about how and why the plethora of Martech tools that are available today came about. We'll also talk about the effort to categorize Martech by Scott Brinker, which brought much spotlight to the concept of Martech. In addition, we'll briefly talk about Scott Brinker's categorization of Martech, and why we opted to create a simpler categorization. We'll then break down the categories of Martech, and list sample tools and platforms in each one. By the end of this chapter, you should have a good handle on the different types of Martech available and what each category does.

How Did We Get So Many Marketing Tools?

There are a few key reasons why there is so much Martech available in the market today. The first reason is budget. Marketing (specifically advertising) has traditionally had a large budget to spend to try to acquire customers and new sales. In fact, according to Zenith, global ad spending was over $705 billion in 2021. Since advertising and marketing services typically have lower overheads than physical products, creating tools and services to help marketers is a profitable business (Zentihmedia.com). The second reason is the rise of different tasks and activities that marketers need to perform to do their jobs. Since marketing is becoming increasingly digital, the number of digital tasks that marketers have to do has increased. For example, launching a campaign requires writing a document, designing graphics, building digital ads and emails, deploying advertisements, tracking and reporting, and much more. To support this growing number of activities, large tech firms as well as entrepreneurial startups have created tools and services and have begun to compete for marketing dollars. The final reason for the Martech explosion is that creating software products has become easier. Most Martech tools are what we call software-as-a-service (SAAS), which refers to a software application that you do not have to download, and typically runs in the cloud. Technology today such as cloud computing (hosting a network of computer servers rather than maintaining servers in a facility on-site) enables new SAAS products to be built faster.

The Cost of So Many Tools

A recent LinkedIn poll of 1100 marketers posed the question, "What is the biggest challenge in Martech today?" The winning response? "High on tools, low on strategy" (Figure 3.1).

This refers to the fact that many companies purchase tools to solve their problems versus coming up with a coherent strategy. While this isn't true for every company, it is important to understand what the purpose of all these Martech tools are for, and how they help marketers achieve their objectives.

FIGURE 3.1 Results of a LinkedIn Poll

What is the biggest challenge in Martech today?

You can see how people vote. **Learn more**

High on tools, low on strategy ✓	**51%**
Lack of skilled talent	**17%**
Lack of integrated data	**30%**
Missing functionality	**2%**

1,142 votes • Poll closed • **Remove vote**

Scott Brinker's Martech Super Graphic

A book about Martech would not be complete without covering Scott Brinker, fondly referred to as "godfather" of Martech, and his compilation of the largest database of Martech tools in the world. Scott founded ChiefMartec.com, a blog and resource center for marketers to understand the Martech space. One of his most famous (or notorious) projects was the Martech Super Graphic. Scott compiled hundreds of Martech tools, categorized them, and put all of their logos onto one graphic. Over the years, the super graphic grew from a few hundred tools to over 8,000 different Martech tools and platforms.

The other helpful part of this project was compiling the list of Martech tools into an accessible database. Scott organized all of the different Martech tools into categories. The categories of Martech outlined in this book are a variation of Scott's categories, with the goal of simplifying the categories for marketers, as well as to segment the tools in a way that is easy to understand.

Martech Categories

In this chapter we will be focusing on the key categories of Martech. We break up the categories into two over-arching themes: **marketing specific** and **marketing collaborative** (see Figure 3.2). The categories (and subsequent tools) in the marketing-specific theme are products that have been developed to specifically support marketers. They are highly unlikely to be used by any other team in the organization. For example, platforms for advertising on social media channels were built specifically for marketers, and are unlikely to be used by any other team. The categories of Martech in the marketing-collaborative theme are platforms that are heavily used by the marketing team but may have not been developed for specifically for marketers. These platforms are also used for similar purposes by other teams in the organization. For example, customer relationship management (CRM) platforms are used by the marketing team to take customer and prospect data to segment marketing efforts as well as to report on revenue data.

FIGURE 3.2 Martech Categories

However, CRM platforms are also used by sales for relationship management, customer success for account management, and finance for forecasting.

Marketing-specific categories:

- Marketing and advertising;
- Content and website;
- Marketing custom (marketing reporting, marketing project management).

Marketing-collaborative categories:

- Sales and CRM;
- Data management;

- Analytics;
- Management and finance.

The Pros and Cons of Marketing-Specific Applications

Pros: The pros of platforms built specifically for marketers is that they are more customized to marketers needs. For example, imagine looking at an email report. With a general data tool, you may get a spreadsheet full of metrics, such as sent, delivered, opened, clicked, and unsubscribed. You would need to work on this data to display important ratios such as the delivery rate, open rate, click-through rate, and unsubscribe rate. In a marketing-specific application, the purpose of the report is to provide these ratios, so all of them would be ready-made for you. In addition, these tools tend to be easier to implement and more affordable, especially compared to enterprise business software.

Cons: The cons of marketing-specific applications are that you can run up against a wall when it comes to sophistication and flexibility. Once your organization matures, you may find yourself needing custom requirements, which marketing-specific applications were not built for. Another con is that marketing-specific applications typically do not integrate with as many other platforms as the marketing-collaborative category. Let's take Salesforce.com, for example, a CRM in the marketing collaborative application categories. Salesforce.com integrates with over 10,000 different tools, while a marketing-specific application would integrate with 10–20 different tools.

Let's start with the marketing-specific categories, beginning with "marketing and advertising."

Marketing Specific: Marketing and Advertising

The first category is **marketing and advertising** (Figure 3.3). This category of Martech tools contains some of the mainstay business cases for marketing, including promotion, increasing awareness, and

FIGURE 3.3 Marketing and Advertising Subcategories

affinity, engagement, and conversion of customers. This category is further broken up into subcategories:

- Advertising and PR;
- Email and marketing automation;
- Social, mobile, and conversational marketing;
- E-commerce marketing;
- Conversational marketing;
- Marketing and advertising;
- Offline marketing.

Advertising and PR

Today's consumer is everywhere—on every channel and digital platform. The tools in the advertising and PR subcategory are designed to drive awareness and action for a brand's products and services. Advertising platforms support the creation, placement, and measurement of ads across a brand's website, owned and operated properties, third-party sites, social media platforms, online content, mobile applications, and more. Today, advertising tools (referred to as AdTech) also encompass newer channels such as influencer marketing and podcast marketing. Public relations (PR) platforms support all of the needs of the traditional PR function, including dissemination of news, earned media, and the management of analysts and journalists.

WHICH TOOLS TO FOCUS ON?

The tools you select from this list will depend on your advertising budget. Companies with a more transactional sales cycle, where most purchases occur online for example, tend to spend more on paid advertising. When this happens, it is important to compare advertising channels and campaigns against each other and optimize ad spend as much as possible. Companies with longer sales cycles typically have smaller advertising budgets, and rely on field sales teams for most deals. These types of companies will be able to get away with a smaller set of advertising and PR tools.

Advertising and PR services include:

- Google Marketing Platform—Advertising, PPC, CPM;
- DisplayOpenX—Programmatic advertising; Facebook Ads;
- LinkedIn Ads;
- Adroll;
- Admob;
- Adcolony;
- SEM Rush;
- Spyfu;
- Adespresso.

Email and Marketing Automation

Some of the biggest platforms that marketers operate are email and marketing automation, and here's why: over 11,000,000 trillion emails are sent every week, and email is one of the most personal and profitable marketing channels. While there are many powerful features included in email marketing platforms such as segmentation and personalization, marketing automation takes email to the next level by including lead management, lead nurturing, events, content download campaigns, and more. In addition, marketing automation platforms typically sync with a CRM platform so the data can inform better campaign targeting, lead lifecycle management, and reporting.

WHICH TOOLS TO FOCUS ON?

Generally speaking, B2C (business-to-consumer) companies will typically use an email marketing platform while B2B (business-to-business) companies will use a marketing automation platform—because of marketing automation's integration with CRM. One strategy is to review the pricing model for each one. If your database size and the number of emails sent falls in the average pricing for a vendor, you are probably on the right track. If your database and volume of emails sent is on the low-end or high-end of the pricing structure, it is a good sign that you should consider vendors that specialize in servicing businesses of your size.

Email marketing platforms include:

- Constant Contact;
- Mailchimp;
- Aweber;
- Campaign Monitor;
- Omnisend;
- Sendinblue.

Marketing automation platforms include:

- Marketo Engage, by Adobe;
- Eloqua, by Oracle;

- Pardot, by Salesforce;

- Hubspot;

- Active Campaign;

- Drip;

- Customer.io.

Social, Mobile, and Conversational Marketing

Tools in the social, mobile, and conversational marketing subcategory focus on mediums beyond the normal website and email engagement. Social media marketing tools support the creation, publishing and scheduling, and reporting of social media campaigns—both paid and organic. In addition, some social media tools focus on social media listening, which helps brands identify important topics and sentiments that their customers are talking about. Mobile marketing tools create campaigns that engage customers on their smartphones and tablets, and include mobile ads, push notifications, and SMS text messaging campaigns. Conversational marketing is new. It describes interacting with customers through live chat and chatbots, typically on a brand's website.

WHICH TOOLS TO FOCUS ON?

Unless you are working at a large enterprise, most of the lower-priced tools in this category should work for your needs. Enterprise companies require customization and high volume, to the point where it will be too much manual effort to manage in a smaller tool. One thing to consider is if you are looking for a specific feature—like an interactive social media experience or chat experience—it may only be available on higher-priced platforms.

Social media tools include:

- Hootsuite;

- SproutSocial;

- Buffer;

- Salesforce Marketing Cloud.

Mobile marketing tools include:

- Vibes;
- Airship;
- Trumpia;
- Mobivity.

Conversational marketing tools include:

- Drift;
- Intercom;
- Livechat;
- Qualified.

E-Commerce Marketing

Software and platforms in the E-Commerce Marketing subcategory focus on driving marketing and sales efforts to increase online sales. The most common example of this is technology to attract visitors to an online store, persuade and nurture them to purchase, and follow up for repurchases.

WHICH TOOLS TO FOCUS ON?
Integration with your website and payment system are going to be the important factors for e-commerce. Focus on streamlined processes, automation, and ease of use for this category.

E-commerce marketing tools include:

- Kissmetrics;
- Omnisend;
- Klaviyo;
- Hotjar;
- CrazyEgg;
- AdNabu.

Offline Marketing

The tools in this subcategory support the traditional forms of non-digital marketing mediums, such as billboards, in-store advertising, and direct mail. They specialize in the creation, customization, personalization, delivery, and reporting of offline initiatives.

WHICH TOOLS TO FOCUS ON?

The vendor you select for offline marketing should depend on your campaign volume needs. In many cases, you can experiment with channels like direct mail on your own, evaluating its effectiveness, and then selecting a vendor based on that performance. Many marketers make the mistake of purchasing a platform that only brings value when there is a large volume of activity that it supports.

Offline marketing tools include:

- Sendoso;
- Alyce;
- PFL;
- Vistaprint;
- Update this.

Marketing Specific: Content and Website

The marketing-specific category of **content and website** is large because so much of digital marketing involves content and website initiatives. Take the website for example. All of your product pages, case studies, blog articles, videos, and how-to resources will live on this site. This is your digital storefront, and the way the world sees your brand online. It's critical for a marketing team to be able to create, publish, modify, and track the performance of their content on and off their website. These tools help attract and convert prospects into paying customers from a website standpoint.

CMS

Content management systems (CMS) are platforms to host files on the internet. This is typically enterprise content, such as different types of documents, scripts, and media files for a corporation, and web content management, which is all the files you need to run and publish on a website. A simple, and common, example is a platform that allows a business to create and manage the company website. A CMS enables a marketing team to create website pages, host images and scripts, host media files like video and other interactive content, and optimize and analyze the performance of a website.

WHICH TOOLS TO FOCUS ON?

For this category, you need to evaluate the skill level of those managing the platform. If you have beginners that will manage it, you should consider a platform that is mostly done for you, with only slight customizations required of your team. More experienced teams will realize the benefits of more robust platforms since they can be endlessly customized.

CMS applications include:

- Wordpress;
- Wix;
- Squarespace;
- Drupal;
- Adobe Experience Manager.

SEO

SEO stands for search engine optimization, and the tools in this subcategory help websites to be discovered on the internet. To accomplish this, these tools help marketers evaluate the overall health of the site, problem areas that could hurt search rankings, and give tips on how to optimize for search engines. This includes optimizing for keywords, checking broken links, and optimizing for technical and SEO content—as well as site speed.

SEO tools tend to be lower cost, and there is little risk to trying them out. Consider trying all of them and finding which ones suits the needs of your team best!

SEO tools include:

- SEMrush;
- Moz;
- Google Search Console;
- Ubersuggest;
- Clickflow.

Content Marketing and Interactive Content

According to the Content Marketing Institute: "Content marketing is a strategic marketing approach focused on creating and distributing valuable, relevant, and consistent content to attract and retain a clearly defined audience—and, ultimately, to drive profitable customer action." (Contentmarketinginstitute.com) Content marketing software and applications help in all areas of publishing, distributing, measuring and optimizing content. In addition, some of these tools help marketers develop interactive content, such as dynamic infographics, quizzes, and more.

Your content marketing tool choice should depend on the volume of content you have. If you have hundreds of content assets such as reports, eBooks, blog posts etc., it pays to invest in a robust platform. For those just getting started, you should consider managing content manually until you start to run into bandwidth issues.

Content marketing tools include:

- Airstory;
- Grammarly;
- Hubspot;

- Contentools;
- DivvyHQ;
- Acrolinx;
- Pathfactory.

Digital Asset Management (DAM)

Digital asset management (DAM) applications help marketers store, manage, and share media files and other documents. Examples of these files are images, PDFs, videos (mp4), and audio files (mp3). While these is some overlap in DAM and enterprise content management, DAM typically refers to files that will be utilized for marketing efforts. The benefits of DAM include being able to quickly locate files and resources; improve asset workflows; increase collaboration among teams; and improve the overall organization and discoverability of assets.

WHICH TOOLS TO FOCUS ON?

Digital asset management tools tend to work better for large teams with many digital assets. Agile teams with less than ten people can get away from using a free/low-cost file storage platform. Once you see issues such as marketers not being able to find resources, or problems collaborating, test out DAM tools with the features that suit your team best.

DAM tools include:

- Brandfolder;
- Bynder;
- Frontify;
- Amplifi.io;
- Canto;
- IntelligenceBan.

Events, Webinars, and Meetings

Online events and collaboration opportunities are more popular than ever. The tools in this subcategory enable teams to create online gatherings of all sizes. While many of us may be familiar with online meeting and collaboration tools, applications today can host thousands in an online webinar, and even tens of thousands in a virtual conference. The tools in this subcategory support the creation and hosting of these events, facilitation of meetings, promotion, measurement, and optimization of virtual gatherings.

WHICH TOOLS TO FOCUS ON?

For most companies, Zoom and GoToWebinar will suit most online event needs, and are very flexible in terms of integrations and automations. Marketers that run sophisticated virtual events or hybrid events should consider reviewing other platforms that have features to support these advanced requirements.

Events, webinars, and meeting tools include:

- Zoom;
- GoToMeeting/GoToWebinar;
- On24;
- Brightcove;
- Webex;
- Cvent.

Video Marketing

From promotional videos to video testimonials, video marketing now plays an important part in the overall marketing mix. The video marketing category contains applications that allow marketers to create, edit, publish, optimize, and measure videos for their marketing efforts.

Again, the volume of video content you have should determine if you should use a video marketing platform.

Video marketing tools include:

- Vidyard;
- Loom;
- Wistia;
- Openreel;
- Vyond;
- VidIQ.

Optimization and Testing

An important part of marketing is optimization and testing. While there is some overlap between this category and the CMS category, tools for optimization and testing tend to focus specifically on experimentation. A common example is running advertising and website experiments such as A/B testing, as well as using reporting insights to continually improve the customer experience.

Optimization and testing tools tend to be lower cost and easy to implement. Consider trying most of these tools and finding the one that best suits your team's needs.

Optimization and testing tools include:

- Google Optimize;
- Freshmarketer;
- VWO;
- Optimizely;
- Omnicovert;
- AB Tasty;

- Convert;
- Convert Experiences;
- Evolv.

Marketing Specific: Custom Marketing Applications (Reporting and Project Management)

In this category, we take all the applications that have been specifically created for marketing teams to solve their issues; however, there are other tools that marketers commonly use to solve these challenges that are in a more general category that we will cover later. For example, there are some project management applications that have been developed specifically for marketers, but many other project management tools have been created for teams of all kinds.

Reporting and Analytics

Marketers often have specific types of reports they run around advertising, website traffic, and social media engagement. Tools in the subcategory of reporting and analytics were created to support these efforts to aggregate data from the variety of channels and mediums, and help marketers analyze the results to make better marketing decisions and investments.

WHICH TOOLS TO FOCUS ON?

Keep in mind that you are going to be choosing between marketing-specific reporting tools and marketing-collaborative reporting tools, which are covered later in this chapter. If you are selecting marketing-specific reporting tools, outline the key reports and metrics you need to see beforehand, and then conduct vendor evaluations to see if they will support the reporting that is most important for your business.

Reporting and analytics tools include:

- Bizible;

- Full Circle Insights;
- Funnel.io.

Project Management

Most marketing ends up being some sort of project, and the work of a marketing team has particular nuances. For example, there is typically a designer, copywriter, and some sort of web publisher involved. Given that this is very similar across marketing teams everywhere, the tools in the subcategory of project management for custom marketing applications focus on project and workflow management for these teams.

WHICH TOOLS TO FOCUS ON?

The most robust project management tools tend to be in the marketing collaborative section, covered later in the chapter. Select marketing-specific project management tools only when it provides custom functionality that will work specifically for your team that other tools don't provide.

Project management tools for marketers include:

- Kapost;
- Functionfox.

Budgeting

The budget of a marketing team is often different than any other team in the business. It tends to be heavily focused on advertising and promotion, and is often difficult to track back to ROI. Compounded by the fact that media and advertising campaigns often take place over time, and are not continuous line items, the marketing budget is pretty nuanced. Tools in this subcategory are specifically developed to help marketers with their budgeting needs.

Keep in mind that most budgeting projects start and end using Microsoft Excel. When your budgeting becomes large and unwieldy, it can become difficult to spot redundancies and streamline opportunities, which should then prompt an evaluation of budgeting tools.

Budgeting tools for marketers include:

- Allocadia;
- Hive9;
- Aprimo Plan and Spend;
- Plannuh.

We are now venturing into the **marketing-collaborative** set of categories. These are applications that marketers use frequently to do their jobs; however, there are other professions and roles that use the same tools. As an example, think about how many different types of professions use Microsoft Word—a tool that was not created for any one job!

The Pros and Cons of Marketing-Collaborative Applications

Pros: The pros of marketing collaborative applications are that you can usually depend on them long-term. These companies tend to have been around longer, are well-funded, and have long future roadmaps which will continue to evolve to support their customers. As previously mentioned, marketing-collaborative applications have more integration partners, and can be customized more than marketing-specific applications can.

Cons: The cons of marketing-collaborative applications are that they are usually more expensive and require great effort to configure and implement. While this isn't always the case, it is particularly true in the categories of sales and CRM; customer experience, service, and success; CDP; and reporting and analytics. Another con is that since these products serve more functions than solely marketing, marketers may end up owning/being responsible for non-marketing activities, which may distract them from their goals.

Marketing Collaborative: Sales and CRM

CRM

CRM stands for customer relationship management. According to Salesforce, "CRM is a technology for managing all of your company's relationships and interactions with customers and potential customers. The goal is simple: Improve business relationships" (Salesforce, 2015). To be more specific, CRM is the system that sales teams manage in order keep track of their accounts, opportunities/ deals, and leads. Today's CRM players are very robust, offering many expansions upon this initial definition, much of which is capturing and organizing data about customers in order to improve sales and marketing efforts. Though there are other new platforms that store customer data, at the time of this writing, many companies still consider the CRM as the "source of truth" when it comes to customer data. Marketers use the data in the CRM for targeting, analysis, and reporting. It is the starting point of many of their marketing campaigns.

WHICH TOOLS TO FOCUS ON?

The market leader in this category is Salesforce.com, and for good reason. The amount of customization and integrations in the AppExchange (app marketplace with over 10,000 partners) make it a solid choice for reliability and scale. Investigate other platforms when you need custom features or when you are tied to specific vendors (for example, it may be easier to procure Microsoft Dynamics if your company is approved to only use Microsoft services).

CRM platforms for marketers include:

- Salesforce;
- Microsoft Dynamics;
- SugarCRM;
- Netsuite;
- Hubspot CRM;

- Zoho CRM;
- Pipeline Deals.

Customer Experience, Service, and Success

Applications in the customer experience, service, and success subcategory focus on improving the service to customers. The functions they support are analyzing and capturing customer feedback, and developing mechanisms to continually drive a delightful customer experience. This can include customer surveys, net promoter score (NPS) measurements, as well as online support resources and forums for customers to get assistance.

WHICH TOOLS TO FOCUS ON?

Zendesk is the market leader in this category, though you can consider Salesforce Service Cloud for more in-depth integrations with your CRM. If you have custom needs or budget, investigate other platforms that may give you an edge over Zendesk users.

Customer experience, service, and success platforms include:

- Zendesk;
- Happyfox;
- Yext;
- Kustomer;
- Salesforce Service Cloud;
- Freshdesk;
- Teamsupport.

ABM

Account-based marketing (ABM) is defined as: "A business marketing strategy that concentrates resources on a set of target accounts within a market. It uses personalized campaigns to engage each account, basing the marketing message on the specific attributes and needs of the account" (Optimizely, 2019). The strategy and tactics around ABM differ from traditional, funnel-based marketing approaches that try to generate as many leads as possible and convert the qualified ones. While there is some overlap between ABM and CRM tools, the applications in this subcategory focus on identifying key accounts, penetrating and engaging target accounts, and reporting on account acquisition and expansion efforts.

WHICH TOOLS TO FOCUS ON?

Make sure you have an ABM strategy in place before you purchase an ABM platform. While vendors may say otherwise, an ABM platform will not magically drive results from ABM for you. Once you have a strategy in place, identify the key parts of that strategy, and talk to each vendor to see how they can support your specific needs.

ABM platforms include:

- Demandbase;
- Terminus Triblio;
- Hubspot ABM Software;
- Marketo Engage ABM by Adobe.

Sales Automation, Enablement, and Intelligence

While CRM is the core platform that sales use, the subcategory of sales automation, enablement and intelligence is designed to help salespeople sell more efficiently and effectively. Because marketing has much oversight and alignment with sales to achieve objectives, marketing is typically the one who owns or is at least responsible for these platforms. The tools in this subcategory include email cadence tools, buyer intelligence, product information and education, and sales training.

WHICH TOOLS TO FOCUS ON?

This category of tools depends heavily on sales preference and adoption. Identify key areas of sales support you want to provide, and work with vendors to have sellers pilot tools and see which ones they prefer. In addition, as with all tools, make sure the prospective tools integrate with the key parts of your tech stack.

Sales automation, enablement, and intelligence platforms include:

- LinkedIn Sales Navigator;
- Outreach.io;
- Salesloft;
- Reply.io;
- LeadFuze;
- PredictLeads;
- Chili Piper.

Call Analytics and Management

Call analytics and management deserves its own subcategory because much of business and deals are made over the phone (or over Zoom). This includes the tracking, recording, and analyzing of sales and customer success call data to drive insights into making the customer experience better.

WHICH TOOLS TO FOCUS ON?

There are only minor differences between the call analytics and management platforms. Compare the features and pricing against each other on a spreadsheet and select the one that works best for you team.

Call analytics and management platforms include:

- Gong.io;
- Chorus.ai;
- Callrail;
- Invoca.

Marketing Collaborative: Data Management

Big data is a big deal, and now we get into the category of data management. I've been quoted as saying "great marketing can't happen without great data," and many of these platforms focus on bringing data to life to achieve marketing objectives.

CDP

According to the CDP Institute, "A Customer Data Platform (CDP) is a packaged software that creates a persistent, unified customer database that is accessible to other systems." A CDP will aggregate data from other sources, standardize and normalize that data, and create a primary customer profile. Once structured, this data is made available to other systems. The business problem CDPs solve is that data is in disparate systems, and it is difficult to get a single view of what is happening with your customer. With a single-customer view, marketers can make better targeting, positioning, messaging, and other value-driven decisions. The types of data that CDPs aggregate range from personally identifiable information to behavioral data such as website activity, as well as product and service usage data.

WHICH TOOLS TO FOCUS ON?

CDPs are a large platform purchase, so you will want to go through a detailed vendor comparison to select the best CDP for you. List out your use cases, desired features, integrations, pricing, and current customers to help make your choice. A detailed look at how to perform a Martech vendor evaluation is covered in Chapter 7.

Customer data platforms include:

- Tealium;
- Segment by Twilio;
- Blueshift;
- Bloomreach;
- Blueconic;
- Amperity.

DMP

Similar to CDPs, data management platforms (DMPs) aggregate data from multiple systems into one place. However, DMPs focus mainly on advertising initiatives, by gathering large amounts of second- and third-party data (usually anonymous) to build audiences for advertising. Though the data is typically anonymous, the DMP solves the challenging business problem of having audience data in multiple platforms and systems.

WHICH TOOLS TO FOCUS ON?

Like CDPs, DMPs are a large platform purchase, so you will want to go through a detailed vendor comparison to select the best DMP for you. List out your use cases, desired features, integrations, pricing, and current customers to help make your choice. A detailed look at how to perform a Martech vendor evaluation is covered in Chapter 7.

Data management platforms include:

- Salesforce Audience Studio;
- MediaMath;
- Oracle Data Marketplace;
- Adobe Audience Manager;
- Adform;
- Latame Data Exchange.

iPaaS

Integration platform as a service (iPaaS) is a platform that helps connect systems together and is described as "a suite of cloud services enabling development, execution and governance of integration flows connecting any combination of on premises and cloud-based processes, services, applications and data within individual or across multiple organizations." (Gartner.com) A great example of this is moving data from one database to another, or triggering actions based on events in separate systems. This is a rising category since Martech stacks are becoming increasingly large in organizations.

WHICH TOOLS TO FOCUS ON?

For small projects, Zapier should work to service your needs. You will need to use platforms like Workato and Tray.io for more sophisticated requirements, and platforms like Mulesoft for enterprise projects.

iPaaS providers include:

- Workato;
- Zapier;
- Tray.io;
- Mulesoft.

Data Enrichment

Data enrichment tools populate missing fields in records in a database. It can take one single piece of data (such as an email address or phone number) and add more data points to the record such as an address, job title, and company information. The benefits of data enrichment are better support for targeting and segmenting initiatives as well as driving customer insights, while improving conversion rates because less information is requested from leads. Most data enrichment services either enrich data in bulk or in real time when a lead fills out a form.

WHICH TOOLS TO FOCUS ON?

Pick data enrichment tools based on the quality of data, platform usability, and pricing. One thing to keep in mind is that different data enrichment vendors excel in different industries. For example, if you are selling to industrial companies or tech companies, some vendors have better data sets that others in those industries.

Data enrichment platforms include:

- Zoominfo;
- Insideview;
- Salesgenie;

- Clearbit;
- Pipl;
- Ringlead.

Governance and Compliance

Governance and compliance is extremely important, and is an often overlooked topic in marketing. The tools in this subcategory include data security, customer consent, customer privacy, protection of personal identifiable information, and more.

WHICH TOOLS TO FOCUS ON?

Applications in this category are highly dependent on the use case, what type of data is involved (for example, whether it is personal information), and what your legal and compliance team needs in terms of features and security.

Governance and compliance applications include:

- Red Marker;
- The Search Monitor;
- Ziflow;
- Compliancepoint.

Marketing Collaborative: Analytics

In this category, we take a look at the tools marketers use to make better decisions. While this is a key aspect of Martech, many other disciplines use these tools to analyze and learn from data.

Reporting and Analytics

Marketers load reporting and analytics tools through a data connection or manually, in order to evaluate the performance of their campaigns, as well as to see any trends or patterns. With today's technology, many of these reporting and analytics tools include machine learning capabilities to help spot trends and patterns.

WHICH TOOLS TO FOCUS ON?

Unfortunately, pricing may be the first determinant in your tool choice in this category, since reporting and analytics tools can be expensive. Once you have narrowed down the vendor list based on what you can afford, consider the depth of analysis you will need to conduct and how easy it will be to perform in each tool. Remember, for early-stage companies without much data, you can get most of what you need from free services.

Reporting and analytics tools include:

- Domo;
- Spreadsheet Server;
- Wrike;
- Dundas BI;
- Prophix;
- Planful;
- Zoho Analytics.

Data Visualization

While there is some overlap with the reporting and analytics subcategory, data visualization tools specialize in creating different forms of charts and graphs, and other visual representations of data. Representing data in different visual formats makes it easier to present and share, as well as can reveal key patterns or trends that we would not see just by looking at numbers in a report.

WHICH TOOLS TO FOCUS ON?

Tableau is the market leader for mid-size to large companies, and besides being incredibly powerful, mastering it is a great skill that can support your career. If Tableau is not on your list due to pricing or talent restrictions, review the common visualizations you will need to perform—as well as number of users—to help select the right data visualization tool for you.

Data visualization tools include:

- Tableau;
- Qlikview;
- Fusioncharts;
- Highcharts;
- Sisense.

Marketing Attribution

Marketing attribution is the practice of assigning credit to positive marketing outcomes. The most common example of this is assigning revenue credit to different types of marketing channels and campaigns. For example, if a deal worth $10,000 closed because of marketing, the credit for that revenue would be assigned to one or more campaigns. The purpose of marketing attribution is to evaluate the performance of each component of a marketing strategy for optimization. The tools in this subcategory support all the efforts needed to accomplish marketing attribution, including tagging, campaign organization, tracking, and reporting.

WHICH TOOLS TO FOCUS ON?

Because marketing attribution does not have a standard agreed upon definition, each of these tools will attribute credit differently. Educate yourself on the different types of marketing attribution, learn how each platform assigns credit, and select the one that works best for your circumstance.

Marketing attribution tools include:

- LeadsRx;
- Dreamdata;
- Factors.ai;

- Singular;
- AppsFlyer;
- Attribution;
- Odyssey Attribution.

Marketing Collaborative: Operations and Finance

Many parts of the business require operations and finance, and the tools in this category assist marketers with these specific objectives.

Project Management and Agile

From a strictly workload perspective, most marketing can be considered project management. Marketers create plans, design assets, collaborate with stakeholders, launch campaigns, and report on success. The tools in the project management and agile subcategory support all areas of project management for marketers. This includes tracking projects and working with cross-functional teams to achieve objectives. Agile is a part of project management that emphasizes shorter work sprints and constant feedback, and there are applications that support work in this style.

WHICH TOOLS TO FOCUS ON?

For small to medium-sized teams, you really can't go wrong with Asana or Trello. These are low-cost project management tools with a wealth of features. Once your needs become larger, and especially as you begin working with technical resources such as developers, investigate Write, Jira, and Workfront.

Project management tools include:

- Asana;
- Trello;

- Wrike;
- Jira;
- Basecamp;
- Monday;
- Smartsheet;
- Workfront.

Budgeting and Finance

The financial aspect of marketing is a big one. The marketing budget is usually one of the most complex and ambiguous budgets in the company, especially when it comes to advertising and ROI. The collection of tools that make up the budget and finance subcategory help marketers manage their finances, forecast spend and results, and ensure proper accounting and tracking of spend.

WHICH TOOLS TO FOCUS ON?

Unless you have a complex marketing budget setup, you only need to onboard a budgeting tool to handle budgeting at scale. Most teams can be well supported with a spreadsheet budget, and keep in mind that you have to submit budget to finance on a spreadsheet. If a budget tool is needed, list out the key features and usability requirements and identify which tools match your needs.

Budgeting and finance tools include:

- Scoro;
- Centage;
- Prophix;
- Float;
- Planguru;
- Adaptive Insights.

Summary

- The Martech landscape is exploding, with over 8,000 different tools to choose from.
- There are two overarching themes of Martech tools: marketing specific and marketing collaborative.
- Marketers need to understand the category of marketing technology and its purpose, and then select from vendors in each category.

04

What is a Martech Stack?

In this chapter, we dive into what it means to build a Martech stack, the key considerations that you need to think about when building it, and the pitfalls that you should watch out for as you build out the marketing technology in your organization.

What is the Definition of a Martech Stack?

A Martech stack or "tech stack" is the entire collection of tools, applications, and platforms that a marketing team uses to achieve their business objectives. Often, the Martech stack will be made up of applications that serve one or more specific marketing functions. For example, a marketing team could have a tool to support email marketing, another tool to support social media marketing, and a tool for reporting and analytics. However, some of the larger Martech platforms serve multiple purposes and encompass several of these functions. The tools in a Martech stack often have data connections and integrations with each other, making marketing more seamless.

One fairly accurate way of determining if a piece of technology is in a Martech stack is if the invoice is paid for from the marketing budget. Tools in a Martech stack typically fall under a technology line item in the budget, or have a line item dedicated to that specific tool. Services that are not included in the marketing budget are usually outside of the Martech stack, even though marketing teams may use the applications frequently. This could be services such as office productivity, storage, and hardware—among many others.

Why Are Martech Stacks Important?

FIGURE 4.1 The Importance of Martech Stacks

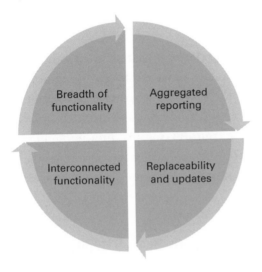

Breadth of functionality: Martech stacks enable marketers to fulfill a host of functions that they need to support in order to engage and deliver value to customers. A collection of tools serving different functions allow marketers to attract, engage, convert, and delight customers. Without Martech stacks, marketers would have limited independent capabilities, and need to rely on other teams to get their work done.

Aggregated reporting: Having a Martech stack helps you track different customer engagement from the different customer touchpoints where they interact with your business. This could be on your website, paid media ads, paid and organic social, email, and other areas. Marketing technology, whether individually or combined, helps aggregate this valuable data, which can be collected and analyzed later.

Interconnected functionality: In addition to having many different functions, Martech also helps create new functionality and marketing value by offering up the option of connecting Martech tools together. For example, by combing a data enrichment platform with a landing page and form, marketers can augment the data they receive from a prospect, while reducing the number of fields of information that they are asking for, therefore increasing conversion. Another example is connecting a marketing automation platform to a webinar platform, enabling emails to be sent to attendees based on audience engagement and participation.

Replaceability and updates: Another great thing about Martech is that it is (usually) easily replaceable and updatable. For example, if you aren't getting the service that you need or results that you expect from a Martech application, it is not too difficult to terminate that subscription and go out looking for another vendor. This also keeps Martech vendors on their toes, as new entrants to the landscape make it so providers must stay up-to-date with features and innovations.

What Does a Martech Stack Typically Look Like?

A Martech stack is essentially a collection of tools, and it is best to look at it in a flow chart or map type format.

The center of a Martech stack will be the larger, main data platforms, this could be a customer data platform (CDP), customer relationship management system (CRM) and/or marketing automation platform (MAP). This could also include a data warehouse, data lake, or other form of place that stores aggregated marketing data. As you move outward in the Martech stack map, you have more function-based tools, such as social media marketing tools, webinar tools, and advertising tools. At the outer parts of the Martech stack you will see the point solutions if any. Point solutions are tools purchased that serve one purpose—and it may be a small purpose.

A Brief Primer—Comparing B2C and B2B Marketing for Martech

This is a common question, and while the principles of marketing are the same for B2C (business-to-consumer) as they are for B2B (business-to-business) there are some tactical differences. First of all, the buying process is more complex on the B2B side. For B2C, a consumer typically arrives at a storefront, whether that is physical or online, and browses inventory. After making considerations by talking to a salesperson or consulting online reviews, the consumer decides on making the purchase or not. B2B is different in that a B2B buyer will learn about a solution either through a problem or through content such as a conference or an industry report. The buyer will then meet with various vendors to compare, and may issue a request for proposal (RFP). The vendors that participate in the official proposal will compete for the buyer's business. In addition, the buyer will typically be one of several members of a buying committee, who will jointly make the decision on what to purchase and with whom. A key point in the difference here between B2C and B2B is the time. Notice how the B2C process is very much accelerated, and takes place over a much shorter timeframe, while the B2B process can take several months or even years to complete.

What Does a B2C Martech Stack Look Like?

The main difference with a B2C Martech stack from a B2B Martech stack is that the center of the tech stack will always be a customer data platform (CDP) or data management platform (DMP); since B2C organizations are storing more consumer behavior and advertising data than B2B organizations. For example, typical B2C brands will be advertising to millions (or even billions) of consumers and this audience data needs a place to live, to be organized, and to be actioned upon. Databases and data management platforms are popular among B2C companies because of this need to manage large audiences. B2C Martech stacks will also have a higher proportion of AdTech or advertising platforms to manage their paid advertising efforts. Since there is typically no direct sales team for B2C companies, much of the marketing and promotion must be done through advertising. We'll also see many more tools dedicated to the creative and social aspects of marketing, since this is important in driving awareness with large numbers of potential customers.

What Does a B2B Martech Stack Look Like?

B2B Martech platforms will have the center of their Martech stack as the CRM or the CDP. For B2B companies, there is usually a direct sales team who manage their prospect and customer relationships in a customer relationship management system, such as Salesforce or Microsoft Dynamics. This is typically the center of the Martech stack, since many of the marketing initiatives are based off of this data. For example, a marketer may want to launch a nurture initiative for prospects that have interacted with their company but have never been converted into an opportunity / open deal. This information, the prospect contact information, and their buying stage is stored in the CRM and therefore is needed to launch the nurture campaign. While historically, the CRM has been the source of truth for B2B companies, more and more marketers are beginning to use the CDP. Because marketers require much more data than sales data or opportunity data to conduct personalized marketing, marketers are turning to the CDP, which stores advertising data and product and service usage data in an accessible and actionable way to support campaigns. The other thing that you will see in a Martech platform for B2B companies is tech that supports field marketing initiatives. These include platforms that help create experiences for live events, webinars, communities and reviews. These are the activities that typical business buyers engage in, and it is important that the B2B Martech stack help facilitate and report on these initiatives.

Martech Stacks Vary in Size

One point to consider is that Martech stacks can be very large or very small, depending on the needs and resources of the business. For example, a non-profit without many resources may have a Martech stack comprised of two or three tools. This can serve them well if it helps them achieve their marketing objectives and helps get their message to their customers/constituents. Large corporations can have many tools that help them execute marketing. Microsoft have claimed to have been using hundreds of Martech applications that comprised their Martech stack. In the case of Microsoft and other enterprises, stacks of this size can often require budgets in the millions of dollars, and require teams of people to operate. Martech stacks also expand and contract based on the needs of the business. Companies experiencing fast growth may add on multiple tools to their tech stack in the course of a few months. Conversely, if a company merges with another, the two companies may consolidate their Martech to avoid redundancies.

What is a Proprietary Martech Stack?

A proprietary (or first-party) Martech stack is when a company builds their own Martech applications, typically bespoke to their needs. This could be the entire Martech stack, or just one specific application. An example of a proprietary Martech platform would be if a company used their internal development resources to create their own database or CRM, rather than subscribing to a third-party tool. It's worth noting that before the explosion of Martech, these "home-grown" applications were very common. These types of proprietary applications are also popular among tech-savvy companies who are pushing the envelope when it comes to marketing and advertising, and they have not been able to identify any vendors to help them.

The Potential Benefits of a Proprietary Martech Stack

First, the functionality and features that your tool has can be fully customized and unique to the needs of your organization. For example, if you need a marketing tool to integrate and populate data in many other internal systems, you can create that from the start. For some organizations, this can be preferable to stringing together a host of applications to accomplish bespoke functionality, or to doing a large amount of custom integration work.

Building Martech internally also has the advantage of having full control of the future roadmap of the technology. If there are features that an organization needs in the future, rather than rely on a vendor to build the features according to their timeline, teams can align resources and prioritize these features.

Another potential benefit is cost. Organizations can save money by building their own tools, especially if they have the development capacity to do so. Rather than pay an ongoing subscription fee, once an internal Martech tool is built, the only ongoing fee would be maintenance and server costs, which should be minimal.

Finally (but importantly) is the potential benefit to security. Data security and customer privacy is becoming increasingly important in the digital age. While many companies place high importance on data security, some vendors do not. In addition, your organization may have higher standards of data security than the typical Martech vendor, and building an internal Martech application offers more control around how data and customer information is protected.

The Potential Challenges of a Proprietary Martech Stack

First, it typically takes long stretches of time to scope, plan, develop, and test new internal tools. While an internal application could take months, or even years to implement, subscribing to a third-party Martech tool can take a few weeks (or even a few days for more agile organizations and for simple use cases).

The next potential downfall is a lack of technical talent, as well as product and development resources to build applications internally. Development typically requires product managers and software engineers, as well as user experience and user interface resources to create. These resources are expensive, and can be particularly difficult to secure for smaller organizations.

Another challenge with proprietary Martech is technical debt. Technical debt has been described as "what results when development teams take actions to expedite the delivery of a piece of functionality or a project which later needs to be refactored. In other words, it's the result of prioritizing speedy delivery or perfect code." (Productplan.com) This is a common problem because external products (those built for external, paying customers) tend to be prioritized over internal products. Development teams may not make every effort to build internal tools in a sustainable, scalable way, and what often results is technical debt. We also see lack of innovation from internal tools. Marketing teams may be tempted to scope internal services just according to their needs and pain points today, but may not be looking years into the future to see what they will need. Despite this, Martech vendors typically excel in innovation, as new features and capabilities helps them sell more subscriptions.

Finally, a lack of integration is a problem with internal Martech tools. While some internal development teams may build open-source platforms that can integrate with other applications, many teams will simply build an internal tool that meets an immediate need. This is a downside, especially compared to some of the mainstay Martech platforms that have created marketplace offerings that connect to hundreds (sometimes thousands) of external applications.

How Do You Put Together a Martech Stack?

These three tools are disproportionately important in a Martech stack: the marketing automation platform (MAP), the customer data platform (CDP), and the customer relationship management system (CRM).

Customer relationship management system (CRM): The CRM is a key component of the Martech stack because it holds prospect, customer, and revenue information. Though not a dedicated tool for the marketing team, the CRM is the starting place for many campaigns. The CRM enables marketers to target prospects and customers based on demographic and firmographic information as well as activity and buyer stage.

Marketing automation platform (MAP): Historically, many B2B companies considered the MAP to be the marketing system of record. This is because all of their prospect and customer data exists in the database of the MAP, and many of the digital interactions can be tracked and aggregated in the MAP. For example, many MAPs track website visits, landing page visits, email engagements, and more, and can tie campaigns to pipeline and revenue data in the CRM. Since many marketing campaigns involve the contact information and assets that exist in the MAP, many marketing teams heavily rely on this piece of technology in their Martech stack.

Customer data platform (CDP): The CDP is becoming an increasingly popular marketing system of record. This is because the CDP extends the capabilities and data of a CRM and MAP and brings it into one unified system. One of the key benefits of the CDP is to take all the different customer data and touchpoints—particularly product usage and advertising data—into one system for better campaign targeting and activation. By starting with customer data, campaign targeting is greatly improved as well as driving customer insights.

The Importance of Mapping and Documenting a Martech Stack

One thing that should be underscored is the importance of mapping and documenting a Martech stack. Documenting a Martech stack refers to writing down (or typing up) all of the different Martech platforms your team uses and using flowchart-style diagrams to show how data moves among them. This is important because it creates an overarching view of all the tools in your stack, their function, and how they work together. Many marketers can become overwhelmed when dozens of applications are in place, with many steps and processes, and data moving back and forth between systems. A Martech stack map shows all the applications in one view, as well as how the data connections are formed among the tools. This also helps to get a view of how customer data journey through your stack. For example, when a customer receives a marketing email, that interaction is reported in the marketing automation platform. The customer clicks through to a landing page, which is stored on a website analytics platform like Google Analytics or Adobe Analytics, and the customer may then fill out their information in a webinar form or other event promotion application. Seeing how this all works visually can help streamline processes and ensure data gets to where it needs to go. An additional benefit is that by mapping and documenting that Martech stack, marketers can uncover patterns and other efficiency opportunities that help drive additional marketing value.

How do you go through the process of mapping and documenting your tech stack? First, you want to start with your largest platforms, typically the ones with most records in the database or that are used the most by the most marketing users and support the most campaigns. Typically, this will be your CRM, MAP, and/or CDP. These should be in the center. Then place your second largest platforms or most-used platforms in a circle surrounding the core platforms. This could be advertising platforms, webinar platforms, and data management platforms among others. Next, you want to draw connecting lines to these different platforms where there is a data integration that exists. This helps you understand how data flows through the different systems in your Martech stack. Continue to make concentric circles around your core platforms until all the tools that your marketing team uses are on the map.

The Importance of Integration in Martech Stacks

One of the things that must be highlighted is the importance of platform integration and data integration in Martech stacks. It has been said that, "Platform integration is a procedure during which the incorporation of various apps and services takes place." (Ikajo.com) In other words, platform integration is connecting one platform to another, and in the case of Martech, it means connecting one Martech application to another. Data integration is similar and has a similar meaning, but specifically refers to taking data from disparate systems and bringing them into one location.

Platform and data integration in Martech is important because it allows the data in disparate systems to be used to improve marketing or to improve insights. To improve marketing, marketers integrate two or more different Martech platforms together to create better offers and/or messages. For example, an online/virtual events platform can be connected to an MAP in order to send attendees (or highly engaged attendees) specific marketing messages via email. The integration of the two platforms creates a better experience for prospects and customers. To improve insights, data from an advertising platform like Facebook or Google can be unified with a CDP to create more granular reporting. In this way, marketers can see which specific customers engaged with specific ads or campaign types. By integrating the data from these various platforms, marketers learn more about their prospects and customers and can make better business decisions.

There are different types of integrations, and an integration can utilize many of the following options. The first is a one-way synchronization, or "one-way sync." This means that the data from one system is being pushed into another system, and the data updates only happen in that direction. The "pushing" system is not affected by changes made to the receiving system. The next is a bidirectional sync, or "two-way sync." This type of sync enables updates to be in both systems. The typical behavior of a bidirectional sync, is that when a record is updated in one system, the connect system updates the corresponding record, and vice versa. Integrations can also be native integrations. This happens when two Martech providers create integration capabilities specifically for each other. For example, Salesforce.com is a popular CRM, and many Martech providers will create a native integration specifically made so that data from their platform can be transferred into Salesforce's application. Another type of integration is custom integration, and this occurs when a business or third party develops an integration for two or more Martech applications. Since custom integrations do not have the oversight of the Martech providers in which the integration is applied, the results can be mixed in terms of effectiveness and accuracy. Note that of the many integrations available, integrations that are native and bidirectional offer the most vendor support and flexibility to support most Martech initiatives.

A Word on App Marketplaces

App Marketplaces (or Application Marketplaces) are directories of tools that integrate with a specific platform. Typically, a large Martech provider will set up and facilitate an application marketplace for all the companies and partners that want to build and sell complimentary services. An example is the app marketplace created by Zendesk. Zendesk is a customer service SaaS solution, which has created an application marketplace of over 500 apps. Different vendors have created these apps to compliment or augment Zendesk functionality. For example, the Zendesk app marketplace has a free tool called Scratchpad, which allows customer service agents to take notes when helping out a customer which they can refer to later. When marketers are selecting Martech providers, they should consider which provider has an app marketplace that they can leverage for future use cases.

Integration Platform as a Service (iPaaS)

Platform and data integration is so critical to managing a Martech stack that applications have been created to service this need. Integration platform as a service (or iPaaS) is a platform that helps connect and unify the data from disparate systems. Before iPaaS, marketers needed to rely on development and engineering resources to build custom integrations. iPaaS often has a collection of ready-made integrations for many Martech applications, allowing marketers to customize these integrations in a drag-and-drop style user interface. For example, the iPaaS provider Workato gives marketers a user interface in which to manage integrations with CRM, MAP, instant messaging tools, and webinar providers, among others.

The Dangers of Manually Updating Systems

It's worth mentioning that many marketers rely on manual efforts to achieve synchronization between systems. This involves download-ing data from one platform and importing it into another. While this may seem like a low-cost, quick fix to data disparity, the data in both systems is never up-to-date for long and can cause greater problems (such as technical debt) down the road.

Who Should Manage a Martech Stack?

With the importance of Martech skyrocketing, it's not surprising to find that Martech requires talented people to manage it. The team that manages Martech is typically known as marketing operations. The marketing operations team is responsible for the tools, processes, and metrics that make executing great marketing work. The tools of marketing are what we think of when we think of Martech—it's the technology that marketing uses to achieve their objectives. The processes of marketing refer to any repeatable set of actions, projects, and approvals that marketing uses to deploy their campaigns and engage their customers. Metrics refer to the effort and deliverables required to measure marketing's performance against objectives and produce insights to help improve marketing decision-making. While this is a large charter that marketing operations is responsible for, in many companies much of the time is spent managing the tools portion, which is also Martech.

What does a marketing operations team look like? While the marketing operations team may vary depending on industry and company size, the core functions remain the same. Whether it's one person managing all of these functions or a team of specialists, the responsibilities of the marketing operations team remains the same.

Tech administration: Martech platforms require a full-time or part-time system administrator. These professionals oversee the system configuration, user roles and permissions, data governance, and usage governance of these platforms. In the example of marketing automation, the tech administrator is often referred to as the marketing automation admin.

Product: The product function consists of product managers, engineers and developers who focus on developing internal products and features to support marketing. This could be building entirely new, proprietary applications, or it could be building integration or feature enhancements to third-party tools. Marketing operations that have dedicated product resources tend to work for larger, enterprise-type companies, but smaller organizations support this function by working with agencies and freelancers, or sharing development resources with other groups within the organization.

Analytics and reporting: There are always members of the marketing team that create and/or support marketing reporting, both at the team level and for the wider organization. These professionals ensure that the different marketing tools and channels are funneling data into a centralized place, and the data is being structured into accessible, actionable reports and dashboards. While it may be helpful for these members to be data scientists or engineers, many data-savvy marketers can assume this role and work with others to support the more technical requirements.

Enablement: Enablement is the stakeholder-facing arm of the marketing operations team. The goal of the enablement role is to make sure stakeholders are adopting and utilizing marketing technology in a way that drives positive business outcomes. The functions of an enablement team focus heavily on training, onboarding, building centers of excellence, governance and policy, and the sharing of marketing best practices throughout the organization.

How to Hire Martech Professionals

Marketers that specialize in managing marketing technology will be the ones taking your tech stack to the next level, so it's important that you identify the right candidates and bring them onto your team. But what do you look for? First, let's consider a question: What makes a Martech professional different than the average marketer? One of the key differences is a strong digital-savvy approach, and an affinity for digital marketing in general. While it is of course possible to be skilled at the many areas of marketing, Martech professionals tend to thrive in digital environments, and can easily pick up digital marketing expertise in search, social, email and mobile. While traditional marketers may be drawn to higher-level strategic marketing concepts such as positioning and messaging, Martech marketers are drawn to the tactical, real-time digital experience of marketing. They also have a strong interest in systems, since marketing technology is primarily made up of connecting systems together, both technical systems and process-related systems. They enjoy learning what makes systems work, and how to optimize systems to efficiently produce more results.

You will also see Martech professionals have a strong "builder mentality," referring to their preference to create innovative products and solutions to pressing problems. While your average marketer may look at a problem and immediately seek out a strategic agency or firm for answers, Martech professionals tend to look at the resources at their disposal and figure out ways to combine and configure technology for a custom solution. Those with builder mentalities still look to others for advice, but enjoy working on problems internally, and in doing so, often invent solutions that have never been considered. In addition, Martech professionals are quickly able to adapt to the extreme rate of change that is forced upon the profession. New channels and platforms constantly pop up, and the interests and desires of the digital consumer are everchanging. Effective Martech professionals deal with this uncertainty by remaining fluid, and by pivoting when necessary or when the data shows that their current approach is not working.

Goals For the Martech Role

Before you start searching for and interviewing candidates, take some time to define what the goals are for the role, and what the expectations for the role will be in the future. Write down clearly what you expect this person to be responsible for, and they will fit into the overall marketing strategy and team. The first key distinction is if this role will need to specialize full-time in marketing technology, or if it will be a hybrid role. Larger organizations, with more resources that smaller ones, will often have specialist roles that devote all of their work to managing and optimizing Martech. This makes sense in that larger organizations will have bigger numbers of tools, data, and users. This translates to more work and labor-hours to manage. Roles that are fully dedicated to Martech also tend to be more technical in nature, for example, large volumes of data may require Martech managers that are versed in data science and able to write basic data programming languages.

Smaller organizations will typically look for and hire hybrid marketers, who work with marketing technology as well as traditional marketing functions. This is for two reasons: one is that there may not be the budget available to hire marketers to work in Martech full-time. Next, there may not be enough high-priority Martech projects to fill those marketers' time. In other words, though there will always be Martech-related tasks to be done, smaller teams would benefit from spending their time on other initiatives. If you determine that the role will be a hybrid of general marketing and Martech projects, it is important that you look for candidates that have the experience and/or aptitude to manage both. If you hire a specialist to work in a hybrid role, and that person has no desire to manage general marketing projects, this could lead to problems down the road.

Another key consideration is what the future of the Martech team will look like. Are you looking to grow this team to several team members, and will the first person you hire be the leader of that team? Or are you looking at an individual contributor role that will not have a team under them for many years? If you anticipate growing the Martech team rapidly to keep up with your own company's growth, or to hit high-growth goals, you should hire a Martech professional that has experience building and managing teams. Hiring an experienced Martech team leader will help share the talent acquisition burden, as well as put the team on a stronger long-term foundation. If you do not have any short-term plans to build out the Martech team, or if you decide that bringing on a leader in the future would be better, you can focus on the specific individual contributor skills during the interview process.

What Skills Should You Be Looking For?

Working effectively in Martech requires a broad mix of business and technical skills. One of the first important skills is an understanding of general marketing management and best practices. If a Martech professionals lacks this knowledge, it likely means that this person will spend time working on the wrong priorities, or not being able to understand the purpose behind implementing platforms and solutions. It's important that Martech professionals understand the purpose of marketing, engaging customers, managing customer lifecycle, and using marketing to drive business results. Next, Martech professionals should have a foundational understanding of data science and analytics. This does not mean that Martech professionals should have a degree in computer science, but since most of marketing technology involves the management and analysis of data, those lacking in this skill are at a severe disadvantage. Marketers in Martech should understand statistics, databases, field types, and other foundational data science concepts.

Another key set of skills is strategic planning and change management. These are often overlooked parts of successful Martech management. Strategic planning is the process of identifying the most important goals for the business or function, and organizing projects and timelines to achieve those goals. This is paramount in Martech because there is a never-ending number of projects that could be tried and tools that could be implemented. It is therefore important for Martech professionals to select the most effective choices to get the job done. Change management is being able to work with various stakeholders to successfully implement new initiatives. For example, it requires change management to stop a team using one marketing platform and start using another. Martech professionals should be skilled in change management because the securing of buy-in for tools and the adoption of tools is one of the keys to making Martech successful. Without a skilled manager in change management, most Martech initiatives will die on the vine.

This stems from another important skill, and that is of the skill of strong communication. Martech managers need to be able to communicate the value of Martech initiatives to leadership and across the organization. For example, many executives don't understand the value of having good data in Martech systems. Skilled Martech managers would explain that good data quality translates to more personalized marketing, better sales handoff, and increased conversion rates, which ultimately will lead to more revenues and profits. These Martech managers are able to get the investments and resources they need to effectively manage marketing technology. An additional communication skill is being able breakdown complex technical topics into understandable information for stakeholders. Many Martech topics are not immediately clear to non-digital marketers, and it's important to be able to communicate the why and the how of Martech platforms in an easy-to-understand way. This enables quick alignment with different groups and can help gain support for the multitude of Martech initiatives that will arise in the future.

What Background Should You Be Looking For?

For senior Martech roles, previous marketing platform experience is highly preferred. Some of the larger Martech platforms such as CRM, MAP, and CDP require more time to learn, and even more time to grasp strategic concepts, so you can save a lot of time by hiring experienced professionals. For more junior-level or entry-level roles, the level of experience does not matter as much. Digital marketing experience is a great indicator of future success in Martech, as digital marketers need to work with Martech frequently, though they may not own or manage the platforms themselves. Digital marketing also requires data analysis and campaign optimization—skills that can be easily transferred to managing marketing platforms. For candidates not coming from a digital marketing background, look for project management experience or experience in operations. The level of detail required to manage projects and to manage the operations of a business translates well into managing Martech.

What Questions Should You Ask Martech Candidates?

What do you enjoy about working in Martech? This is a great question, because Martech managers should be interested in the profession of Martech, and what it can do to drive results for the business. Those that are interested in the profession will continually look at ways to improve Martech, and will always be on the lookout for new strategies and technologies to engage customers and produce results. Look for answers such as the desire to build solutions, integrate tools, analyze data, and use technology to improve the customer experience. Less favorable answers would be if the candidate was relegated to the role of Martech because they could not secure any other type of role, or because no one else wanted to perform the function.

What do you look for when purchasing Martech? This question gives insight into the strategic aspect of how a candidate selects Martech, and the reasoning behind the choices. Martech should serve strategy and should help teams achieve their goals. Look for candidates that think about the overall goals for the business and how Martech supports it, and then look for answers that indicate long-term planning and future-proofing the tech stack. Be wary of candidates who do not put any thought into selecting Martech carefully.

What are the key things to think about when managing a Martech platform? This question indicates how the candidate thinks of the big picture of Martech, as well as how to keep priorities and projects organized. This also gives you a sense of how much experience the candidate has in managing marketing tools. Look for candidates who give thought to integration, adoption, and ROI. Martech professionals should be managing tools with the intent of continually driving high-value business outcomes. Be cautious of candidates who treat managing Martech as just a list of to-do items that need to be accomplished.

What key things do you consider when reviewing marketing reports and marketing system reports? This question gives insight into how the candidate thinks about data, Martech effectiveness, and overall marketing effectiveness. While an average candidate may be interested in increasing basic metrics such as open rates and conversion rates, stronger candidates will be interested in marketing contribution to the business as a whole, campaign ROI, and Martech ROI.

Sample Martech Manager Job Description

The Martech manager will work with various stakeholders across the business to develop and manage a marketing technology stack that helps create exceptional customer experiences and drive positive business results for the organization. This role will be responsible for setting the long-term vision of the tech stack; identifying the right tools and technologies to achieve marketing success; and measuring and reporting on Martech success.

Qualifications:

1 X years in Martech management (or relevant experience).

2 Experience across a multitude of marketing platforms such as marketing automation, CRM, CDP, advertising tools, data enrichment services, and customer engagement platforms.

3 A proven track record in leading marketing platform implementations and/or migrations.

4 Ability to solve complex customer and business problems using technology.

5 Experience working cross-functionally with stakeholders in sales, marketing, customer success, finance, product, and executive leadership.

6 Experience training users on how to best utilize marketing technology.

Preferred:

1 Experience in specific marketing platforms, such as [list out relevant technology here].

2 Certifications in specific marketing platforms, such as [list out relevant technology here].

3 Proficient in project management and program management.

4 If applicable, experience in data science and data visualization.

5 Proven ability to lead large change management initiatives across a global organization.

6 Strong written and verbal communication skills.

The Potential Pitfalls of Building a Martech Stack

While planning and building a marketing technology stack can be an exciting undertaking, there are many things that can go wrong along the way. Be wary of the following pitfalls when building your tech stack.

Shiny object syndrome: Shiny object syndrome is when marketers are attracted to the latest tool, channel, or platform just because it is new. For example, this could be a new, untested social media channel, tactic, or in our case, a marketing application. The danger of shiny object syndrome is that it can lead your overall marketing strategy astray, or at worst completely derail what you are trying to accomplish. Shiny object syndrome is a symptom of one of the deeper, pervasive problem for marketers, which is when marketers let technology drive strategy, versus the right way—which is to let strategy drive technology.

Shelfware: Shelfware is a play on words, and it refers to technology that is not used and remains on the metaphorical shelf. This can be one of the consequences of shiny object syndrome, or simply poor planning and enablement. A common example would be a new Martech application that was purchased by a single marketer, without getting buy-in from the larger team, and subsequently sometime later the application remains unused. Shelfware is not only is a waste of money, but can be very demotivating as stakeholders will be reluctant to try new tech in the future, citing the previous shelfware example as precedent.

Not having the right talent in place: Unfortunately, many business leaders (and even some marketing leaders) don't understand that Martech requires expertise. The implementing and proper management of Martech requires skill and due diligence. This is especially the case for some of the larger Martech platforms like MAPs, CDPs, CRMs, and analytics tools—which require a technology specialist who has prior experience. If a team is unable to secure this talent in-house, it's highly recommended to search out a consultant or agency to assist in Martech implementation. Without the proper technical know-how, Martech is likely to become shelfware, or worse, create a poor experience for customers and stakeholders.

Not understanding that Martech implementation takes time: How long would you say it takes to implement a new Martech platform? How about to complete a Martech migration from one platform to another? Would it surprise you to know that at the enterprise level, projects of this scope and scale take—at minimum—six months to complete? While more aggressive timelines can be met, the best implementations are well scoped and planned, with much input from stakeholders along the way. Moving too fast when it comes to Martech leads to poor implementations, missed deliverables, and technical debt.

The dangers of inconsistent and disparate data: One of the often-overlooked problems that Martech managers face is inconsistent and disparate data. It's natural, especially in a multi-layered Martech stack with dozens of tools, to have data in different places. When the collection, hygiene, normalization, and formatting of the data is different in each system, this leads to data inconsistency. When data is not consistent across platforms, it can impact targeting (uncertainty around who to send/deliver to) and reporting (differing/unreliable cross-system metrics). Data inconsistency compounds over time, so it's best to ensure you have a plan to capture data in a consistent way, and to consistently make efforts to standardize the data.

Decentralized Martech: For larger companies, especially multinational organizations, it is tempting to decentralize marketing technology. This means that Martech is owned by different groups and/or regional offices. The two main challenges with this are redundancy and poor customer experience. Without centralized oversight into which Martech tools a business is leveraging, teams may buy duplicate tools that serve the same function. This can be done out of minor preference reasons (one team likes the user interface of one tool versus another) or can simply done because there isn't knowledge of an existing tool that will suit their needs. Decentralized Martech can also lead to a poor customer experience because of disparate data. Let's say, for example, that one email marketing tool has a record in their database marked as "customer," and another email marketing tool has that same record marked as "prospect." The same customer may then receive customer emails and prospect emails, serving up a very disjointed and frustrating experience.

Shadow IT: Shadow IT refers to when employees purchase technology that hasn't been approved by IT. In Martech, the same occurs when marketers (or sometimes salespeople) purchase Martech without the knowledge of the team that is responsible for all the technology. While there is some overlap between this pitfall and the decentralized Martech pitfall, shadow IT is especially tricky because the Martech team may never know about the existence of tools, and may never have the opportunity to monitor for compliance, security, and customer experience impact.

How Do You Avoid Potential Pitfalls?

We'll get into this in Chapter 5, but in short, having a thoughtful Martech strategy with buy-in from executive leadership will overcome most of these challenges. When strategy drives technology, and you have the support from cross-functional leaders, Martech managers have the authority to exercise the governance that is required when building and enabling an effective tech stack.

A Note About Sales Tech and Sales Automation

It's worth noting the growth of the sales technology space, which includes sales automation / cadence tools that allow salespeople to operate as "mini marketers." While some may not see this as "officially" Martech—because these tools allow sales to reach many people at once—it's important that marketing manage these tools and touchpoints. The best option would be for the Martech team to assume ownership of these tools, and to deploy many of the governance strategies outlined in this book. If this isn't possible, marketing should partner with sales and sales operations to ensure customers are receiving a respectful, thoughtful customer experience regardless of the tools being used.

Summary

- A Martech stack is all of the tools that marketers own and/or use to achieve their business objectives.
- Martech stacks can vary greatly in size depending on the size and type of organization.
- It's important that Martech stacks are integrated to ensure data flows between the business and the customer.
- Marketing operations is typically the marketing function that is responsible for Martech.
- You should be selective about the talent you bring onto the Martech team.
- There are many pitfalls you should watch out for when building a Martech stack, including selecting "shiny new tools" and purchasing tools that you will not use.

05

The Framework for Effective Martech Stack Design

What is Effective Martech Stack Design?

The goal of effective Martech stack design is three-fold. First, marketers need a technology stack that will help marketing achieve their objectives and create great customer experiences. This means that the variety of tools in this internal ecosystem should have the functionality to support marketing efforts. Next, an effective Martech stack helps drive efficiency through a marketing organization. Efficiency refers to both the Martech workflow and the Martech data flow. In terms of workflow, marketers (and other stakeholders) need to be able to access and utilize the various applications in the tech stack. A tech stack where no one can log on or figure out how to use it is a very inefficient tech stack. In terms of Martech data flow, data needs to be able to move between platforms to support marketing initiatives, such as targeting and reporting. Major inefficiency occurs when data is siloed in one platform, or when significant effort is required to pull together reports from many disparate systems. Finally, an effective Martech stack is well-utilized, leading to Martech's return on investment (ROI). It's important that marketers use the tools in the Martech stack and get the most out of it, otherwise the Martech budget is essentially going to waste. Martech adoption is ensured by well-planned onboarding and training programs, and consistent monitoring and usage reporting.

The Principles of Effective Martech Stack Design

There are overarching principles to keep in mind when designing an effective Martech stack: customer journey, benchmarking, simplicity, data integration, and unified reporting (Figure 5.1).

Customer journey: The collection of tools within the Martech stack should be organized around the customer journey. This means that marketers should map out the different stages and touchpoints of their customers' path, from awareness to advocacy. The focus of Martech should be to improve the customer experience (in turn, improving the conversion rate and overall revenue value of each customer) in each stage of the journey. For example, a typical customer journey could be mapped out into these stages: awareness, consideration, evaluation, purchase, and advocacy. Marketers should list out the different touchpoints in each of these stages and ask, "Do we have the right technology to create great customer experiences at each touchpoint?" As an example, let's say we want to improve the conversion rate on a purchase page, which takes place in the purchase stage of the journey. Marketers can leverage an A/B testing tool to experiment and determine which copy, layout, and data help potential customers become more comfortable and willing to become a paying customer.

FIGURE 5.1 Principles of Effective Martech Design

Benchmarking and industry standards: Another key principle to keep in mind when designing an effective Martech stack is to compare to industry leaders, power users, and innovators in the marketing industry and in specific industries. For example, when selecting a data enrichment platform, there is value in learning what top companies use for data enrichment, and how they weave date enrichment in their own Martech stack. This is also true for peers in similar industries and for power users and innovators. There are many benefits to learning about and considering the best practices of others in a similar industry. First, marketers are able to look ahead at how different companies are using a particular technology at scale and over a longer period of time. This is helpful, because marketers usually conduct a trial or pilot to get a sense of how a tool will work for them, but the time period is so short that it is difficult to get some of the data they need.

Next, marketers can avoid potential pitfalls of implementing a Martech tool by learning from others' mistakes. Marketers generally go through a period of trial and error with any new technology, so it is advantageous to learn from the mistakes of others to save time and resources.

Lastly, one of the benefits of following best practices (and sometimes best-of-breed Martech vendors), is that marketers can benefit from the growth and innovation of these services. Many top Martech vendors continue to add new features, integrations, and overall great services that marketers can benefit from and use to engage their customers.

Simplicity over complexity: Another key principle to effective Martech stack design is to build for simple, straightforward solutions compared to complex, multistep solutions. It is better to have a platform that can support three functions well, compared to having three separate solutions and connecting them together. The first reason for this is because Martech stacks tend to become more complicated overtime. The amount of data increases, the number of users increases, and subsequently the volume of requirements placed on marketing increases. Therefore, it is easier to administrate a smaller, simpler Martech stack versus a larger one. Marketers will benefit from starting simple, adding complexity over time as needed.

Second, a simpler stack can be managed by a leaner team. Simplified tech stacks are easier to document, and user permissions are easier to facilitate if there is a smaller set of tools. This also includes training, as each additional tool requires each member to be trained and onboarded.

Third, having a simplified tech stack leaves less room for error. More moving parts and multilayered components create more opportunities for configuration error, user error, and data problems. For example, if data moves between system to system, each additional step is a chance for the data to be changed or corrupted, potentially sabotaging a marketing process.

Data integration: In a LinkedIn poll of 438 marketers, 56 percent said that their top criteria in selecting a new Martech vendor was "available integrations" (Figure 5.2). This underscores the importance of having a Martech stack that has solid connections throughout.

Martech stack designers need to think about data integration and data flow from the beginning. This refers to how data will move between different platforms, and if the synchronization will be one-way or two-way. It is critical for the right marketing and customer data to be able to travel between platforms, as all marketing initiatives require data to be accessible and actionable. For example, marketers need to be able to email webinar attendees before and after an online event, and record attendee engagement in a CRM. Therefore, it is important to select the right webinar, email, and CRM platforms that natively integrate together, or at minimum have open application programming

FIGURE 5.2 Results of LinkedIn Poll

What is your top criteria when selecting a new Martech vendor?

You can see how people vote. **Learn more**

Available Integrations ✓	56%
Innovation and New Features	25%
Customer Service	14%
Community Support	5%

438 votes • Poll closed • **Remove vote**

interfaces (APIs) so that integration is possible. Problems with data integration will slow marketing teams down, and at worst impact their ability to communicate with customers in a timely, relevant way. When possible, marketers should elect to use platforms with a two-way or bidirectional sync, allowing data updates to happen in both directions between systems, helping data stay fresh and actionable in real time.

Unified reporting: Another overarching principle to keep in mind when designing an effective Martech stack is unified reporting. Unified reporting is when the important customer touchpoints and revenue data is brought together to create accurate business reports and dashboards. For example, the data from a website analytics tool, email marketing tool, and CRM should be aggregated in one place to run analysis and build reports. While it is possible to manually download data from separate systems, this method is cumbersome and often inaccurate. When selecting the components of a Martech stack, ensure the platforms can integrate with each other, either natively or through a custom integration.

What Does an Ineffective Martech Stack Look Like?

The signs of an ineffective Martech stack are easy to spot. When any of the following characteristics describe a tech stack, there is great room for improvement.

Incomplete: When marketers are lacking the technology to achieve their objectives or create a desired customer experience, this means that the Martech stack is incomplete. While some marketing teams may have to deal with an incomplete stack for a short period of time (for reasons such as lack of budget or talent), the long-term impact of an incomplete Martech stack can be damaging to business efforts.

Redundant: A lack of a cohesive strategy as well as poor communication among groups often leads to redundancies in marketing technology. One region may have a social media listening tool, while another region may have the same tool or a tool that supports the same function. This results in a waste of the marketing budget, and opens up the marketing team to creating a disjointed customer experience.

Not connected: As mentioned previously, it is important for data to flow through each component of the Martech stack in order to support customer engagement initiatives as well as customer insights and reporting. Data that is isolated in one platform and/or is challenging to utilize with other platforms leads to marketing inefficiency.

Underutilized: Another sign of an ineffective Martech stack is underutilization. This means that the intended users of marketing tools are not using the designated tools that they are supposed to be using. Underutilization leads to shelfware. While lack of training is a common cause of underutilization, another big offender is a lack of purpose and mission behind the Martech tools. There are times when a Martech purchaser will subscribe to a Martech application because of several perceived benefits, but because the Martech buyer did not get feedback from actual users, the tool addresses a need that wasn't quite there.

How Do You Determine the Most Important Functions that Martech Needs to Support?

Before building out a Marketing technology stack, it's important to map out the critical functions the technology needs to support. Marketing teams need to think about three things: the overall business objectives, stakeholder requirements, and the customer experience.

Overall business objectives: In listing out the critical functions that Martech needs to support, marketers should surface the key motivations and drivers of marketing and business leadership. For example, which is first priority—acquiring new customers or cutting-costs? Should the business focus on net-new customer acquisition or expanding upon their existing set of accounts? Does the business have a large sales team that requires many sales enablement tools to facilitate? Is the business largely driven by a self-service funnel that requires many optimization and testing tools? Determine the answers to these questions to list out the key functions your Martech team needs to support.

Stakeholder requirements: While the above emphasizes getting functions from business leaders, stakeholder requirements are received by interfacing with internal customers. Stakeholders include marketing counterparts, sales, operations, customer success, finance, and many others. An effective way to gather the requirements you need is a two-prong approach of workshops and an internal intake system. Hold regular workshops—ideally once a quarter—and invite all relevant stakeholders to review objectives, roadmaps, and to share their requests for the functions and tech they need to do their job. Workshops are particularly good at getting answers to open-ended questions and getting a real taste for the sentiment your stakeholders feel about the projects and workflows that impact them. Next, create an internal intake system, which is a standard process for any relevant stakeholder to submit requests about what they need and the goals they are trying to achieve. While stakeholder requirements are important to meet regularly, remember that they cannot be prioritized over conflicting goals from the overall business and leadership.

Customer experience: Focusing on the customer experience is a great way to stay ahead of the curve when it comes to marketing technology (and when it comes to business in general). By thinking of all the ways a customer interacts with the business—whether it be by website, phone, text, or email—and identifying gaps and ways that technology can improve the experience, marketers can always ensure that they are investing in the right things. For example, it's important to find out if customers and potential customers are easily navigating the company website and getting the information they need. Marketers can assess this question by using website analytics tools such as a heatmap and A/B testing application to monitor customer behavior and make adjustments where necessary.

Different Approaches to Building a Martech Stack

There isn't one single method to build an effective Martech stack. Marketers should be aware of the different paths they can take to mapping out their technology and pick the best fit for their organization.

Lean Organizations: Zero-Based Budgeting (ZBB)

The first approach is great for smaller organizations with a small budget. The lean zero-based budgeting (ZBB) approach is based on teams "starting from scratch" in a new year and identifying the costs absolutely necessary to achieve their objectives; comparing them to the previous year's budget. With this approach, a marketing team takes a look at the key functions they need in order to engage customers, manage marketing overall, and add the tools they need in one-by-one. For example, if a marketing team decides they need website management, email marketing, and a reporting platform to support their function, then they will start with a content management system (CMS), email service provider (ESP), and an analytics tool as their stack. Subsequently, they will look at their budget and secondary needs, and add on as needed. For example, in their plans or throughout the year, they may realize that a webinar platform would be beneficial to have to support their online events. Upon determining if there is available budget for this purchase, the team would onboard a new webinar vendor, or make a business case to justify more budget to be added. This lean approach, while more in line with smaller organizations, can be used by any business to keep costs low and to remain agile.

Enterprise Ecosystems: Jobs-To-Be-Done (JTBD)

The next approach aligns more with larger, enterprise-type companies with more budget and larger resource needs. In the jobs-to-be-done (JTBD) approach, a marketing team will outline all the functions it needs to meet throughout the year. Once complete, an inventory and audit are conducted to outline the current list of marketing technology, with a line drawn to each required function (or "jobs-to-be-done"). This process will identify any gaps in the current system architecture, and allow marketers to earmark budget to purchase the needed technology (which is covered later in this chapter). For example, let's say part of the mapping process shows that the company already subscribes to a marketing automation platform (MAP), customer data platform (CDP), and video marketing application. For this section, the jobs-to-be-done may contain lead nurturing, data normalization, video marketing and data enrichment. Since data enrichment is missing from the existing tech stack, the marketing team will embark on a research and/or RFP process to acquire a data enrichment service. This approach works effectively for large teams that need access to a specific set of tools to accomplish their objectives.

Hybrid Approach (Custom/Iterative)

It's important to consider a hybrid approach for an organization, especially in today's dynamically changing marketplace. A hybrid approach is a mixture of the first two approaches and focuses on an iterative nature of managing your Martech stack.

Select key platforms: Similar to a lean approach, a marketing team using the hybrid approach to Martech stack design should select the major platforms it will use for marketing. However, rather than selecting platforms they think they could not live without, this approach advocates choosing platforms that can help their team gain competitive advantage. This means that a team will review their industry, market share, positioning, and talent and resources to determine which marketing platforms will give them the edge over their competition. For example, companies with strong PR and a good social media presence can emphasize tools that enable them to produce and publish very quickly and repurpose content through a variety of different channels. SproutSocial.com, for example, is a multichannel social media management platform, providing many of these services in one place. This makes it a great choice (albeit more expensive than other social media services) for teams looking to invest in their social content.

Competitive advantage: The idea of competitive advantage also applies to selecting secondary or tertiary platforms to the tech stack. A marketing team should review potential Martech services with the question: How can this platform help tip the scales in our favor? For example, if an organization has a mature field sales organization compared to the competition, selecting Martech that can enable salespeople to accelerate their time-to-value can help the organization solidify its place as market leader. Conversely, for small upstarts looking to unseat the market leader, they may want to invest in innovative channels to engage their audience on a more personal level. Direct mail gifting platforms such as Sendoso, Alyce, and PFL offer up automated ways to send personalized gifts to customers and prospects, emphasizing a different way to contact customers if organizations are unable to compete with a large, direct sales force.

Iterate: While iteration should be part of all Martech design approaches, it is especially important in the hybrid approach, as teams should be constantly evaluating technology that will give them the competitive advantage. On a quarterly basis, marketers should ask themselves these questions: Do we have the right marketing technology to achieve our objectives? Does our existing Martech stack help us keep a unique advantage over our competition? What additional tools are in the marketplace that would allow us to engage our customers and jump a step ahead of the competition? The answers to these questions will be quite revealing, and it is not uncommon to switch out platforms that are satisfactory, for new platforms that will help drive even more business results. The concept of interaction also applies to using existing technology in different ways to optimize marketing, which we will explore in a later chapter.

How to Select Key Martech Platforms?

Especially for the mainstay marketing technologies—such as MAPs and CRMs—there are many great choices in the marketplace. Large Martech vendors and services have been around for more than a decade, and have since created robust and scalable platforms that service almost every industry. While choosing any of these platforms may support the functions a marketing team needs, there are key principles that help ensure you are selecting the right technology for your team.

Budgeting and ROI potential: This may seem obvious, but it's important to select Martech platforms that are in your budget. There are two aspects to this, hard-budget items and ROI potential. Hard-budget items refer to scenarios where purchasing a specific Martech platform is not possible due to financial reasons. Some platforms charge in the hundreds of thousands of dollars per year, and for a small, lean teams this can be a difficult purchase. While it is possible to build a case for more budget, it is best to evaluate technologies that a team can reasonably afford. The next concept is ROI potential, which can be used by any size of organization. ROI is calculated by subtracting the cost of the investment from the sales of the investment and dividing the result by the original cost of the investment. Calculating ROI from a Martech platform can be tricky, because there are likely other factors at play. The key is to attribute and isolate specific sales or gains from the Martech tool. For example, if purchasing a project management tool allows your team to produce twice the number of campaigns, you can count the sales attributed to the additional campaigns in your ROI calculation. ROI potential is one of the fundamental methods to asking and receiving more marketing budget.

Online and offline reviews: Unbiased reviews can help marketing teams decide on the right Martech platform for them. Review aggregation sites like G2Crowd and Capterra collect reviews from users across the globe and generate a review score for easy comparison. Many reviews offer real insight from users who have purchased a specific tool and can offer great insight that Martech vendors won't share. In addition to online reviews, Martech buyers can learn much from talking to their peers. Participating in a quick phone call or Slack community chat can be very helpful, as marketers can ask specific questions around use cases or custom integrations. Many online communities and forums have dedicated channels to discuss the pros and cons of specific marketing platforms.

Future state, scalability, and stability: Marketers need to look 1–5 years down the road and consider if the Martech selections they make today will be the right ones in the future. To do this, analyze decisions from the future state of the business and the future state of the Martech service provider. For future state, ask these questions: Who will our customers be 1–5 years in the future? What channels will we be promoting on? What volume of campaigns will we deploy? What volume of data will need to be analyzed and reported on? Take the answers to these questions and compare them to each tool in the Martech stack. In terms of scalability and stability, it is important that your Martech vendors will be able to support the size and scale of your marketing needs in the future. For scalability, ask: Does the Martech vendor support customers at the future-intended size and scale? Do they support the volume of campaigns that we anticipate deploying? Can they support our data needs when the time comes? For stability, ask: Is the Martech vendor sufficiently funded? Are they in a growth phase or decline phase? What does their future roadmap look like? How would a merger or acquisition affect the services they provide? The Martech landscape is rapidly changing, with many platforms disappearing on a monthly basis. Make sure the vendors you work with will be around to support your marketing needs in the future.

Be Wary of the "Bleeding Edge"

In technology, the "bleeding edge" refers to hardware or software that is not yet fully tested and used by the greater public. These are new, innovative solutions that have been taken on by early adopters, but may have unintended and dangerous consequences, hence the word "bleeding." While it is important to have a culture of experimentation and innovation, marketers should be wary of using applications that could result in a poor customer experience or poor stakeholder experience. For example, if a marketer leverages a new tool that uncovers potential customer contact information, and engages them rapidly and frequently, the result could be positive results in the short-term, but poor customer experience in the long-term. With the advent of privacy and data compliance regulations such as GDPR, new tactics that are potentially underhanded can result in disaster. While this is an extreme example, marketers should still be careful when trying out untested platforms and marketing applications.

Trials and Pilots

One of the most effective ways to select marketing technology is through free trials or small pilots. This offers a low-cost way to see if the tool will work in the way that the vendor describes, as well as see if it will work for the users in your organization. A free trial is when a software vendor offers use of their product or service for a limited time without having the customer pay for it. Free trials vary on usage limits and feature capabilities. For example, some free trials may cap usage or only allow certain features to be used. A pilot is typically a full implementation of the product or service for a much shorter time period than is required of a full commitment. For example, a vendor that typically charges $12,000 annually can offer a one-month pilot where the customer would pay $1,000 for full use of the service with the option of cancelling at the end of the pilot period. Free trials and pilots also enable marketers to test integrations with existing tools in their stack to ensure compatibility and data flow. If the new platform does not integrate well with other tools, marketers can cancel with minimal risk. Another benefit to free trials and pilots is Martech managers can see if their stakeholders can adopt and use the new platform without any problems. Underutilization is a large problem among Martech platforms, and a trial can offer a low-cost way of testing the adoption waters. While there are a host of benefits to free trials and pilots, don't forget about the opportunity cost. Any new tool implementation will take away time for all the users involved, especially the administrators and implementers. Marketers need to be strategic about the free trials and pilots that they elect to participate in, even if there is no monetary fee.

The Worst-Case Scenario Test

Before buying a new Martech platform, it's important to consider the ramifications of the worst-case scenario. If everything goes wrong with this new technology, how can we back out? Some Martech providers insist on lengthy contracts, which can be deleterious if the tool doesn't work out as expected. Ask these questions to prepare: What is the refund policy? Can we cancel our contract early? How fast can we use the next best alternative? As outlined earlier, much of these risks can be mitigated by researching and utilizing peer reviews, but it's always good to have a backup plan. If there is no way out in a worst-case scenario, make sure you factor that into your decision-making.

Time and Talent to Manage

One of the often-overlooked aspects to Martech selection is making sure you have both the time and talent resources to get the most out of a particular tool. Many marketers mistakenly believe that simply purchasing a new technology will solve their problems and drive results. This couldn't be further from the truth. At the enterprise level, for example, large marketing automation platforms and content management systems require entire teams to administrate. In addition to having the people with the bandwidth to manage these applications, you also have to ensure you have the right technical talent. Martech management is on the more technical side of marketing, and while you don't necessarily need engineers or developers, you should have digitally savvy professionals with the experience to facilitate technology. There are many horror stories of companies that have paid hundreds of thousands of dollars for robust marketing platforms, only to have the technology sit there unused for months while the company searches for the right talent to manage it. A good principle to ensure you are ready is that every marketing platform should have a product owner, administrator, and sponsor. A product owner is the person responsible for the contract, support issues that arise, and ensuring the company is getting ROI from the tool. An administrator is responsible for the day-to-day operations of the platform, as well as supporting and governing users. A sponsor is usually a leader or executive that believes in the tool and can weigh in if there is any reluctance to use or implement it. Ensuring you have a product owner, administrator, and sponsor before purchasing a new platform can save you a lot of time and heartache.

Sunsetting/Deprecating Components of Your Tech Stack

Whether it is because you are replacing a platform or no longer getting ROI from it, there will be times when you need to "sunset" or "deprecate" a Martech tool. This refers to the process of stopping usage of a system entirely by all users and all connected systems. First, outline all the use cases and benefits that the soon-to-be deprecated platform provides your company. This could be sending emails, generating reporting, and hosting content. After listing them all out, put together a plan to support these functionalities for the corresponding users after the platform has been discontinued. The future plan of support could include moving to a different technology, or could be an alternative way of accomplishing the same thing. At times, there may be no plans to continue supporting a specific use case, and you will have to clearly document the reasons for that, since there may be some users who complain about lost functionality. Next, make sure to take a look at all the data pipelines the soon-to-be deprecated tool has into other systems. Common ones include data integrations with CRM, MAP, event platforms, and reporting tools. Some reports, for example, may error or cease to function once the "sunsetted" platform stops sending data, so it's best to have a plan to handle those reports beforehand. Once you have a plan for all data pipelines, come up with a timeline for the deprecation that is clearly communicated to all relevant stakeholders. Make sure to include the date of the deprecation, the reasoning behind it, and the next steps they need to take to continue to perform functions necessary for their jobs. Don't underestimate the value of clear communication!

Potential Problems with Martech Stacks

Regardless of how well you design a Martech stack, there are always problems that arise that you undoubtedly need to address:

Steep learning curve: Robust platforms can be hard to learn for marketers. Though marketers are becoming increasingly savvy with digital technologies, they still fall far behind our technical counterparts in IT and engineering. Without a clear learning path and ongoing support, some marketers may never fully get the hang of a new Martech platform, which leads to lack of adoption and shelfware.

Unsanctioned use cases: Many organizations—especially those at the enterprise level—must deal with the problem of marketers using technology in unintended ways. For example, a Martech tool that was meant for hosting simple landing pages can become a major platform in which marketers host all their content. They may do this because the landing page tool is easier to use compared to the designed content management system. This can create cost and functionality issues as certain tools aren't meant for high volume or non-standard use cases. This makes it especially tough to govern and can spell out trouble if marketers are using platforms in ways that violate contract terms or compliance regulations. To avoid this issue, make sure to clearly document and communicate what a Martech application is for, and what it should not be used for.

Service outages: Even the largest Martech platforms go down temporarily. This occurs when an issue (usually server or processing-related) causes marketers to lose access to the platform, or for hosted assets or campaigns to stop functioning entirely. This can be more common with specific vendors than others. To address this, make sure you have a backup plan and a communication plan. The backup plan will outline the steps you will need to take to use an alternative service to support marketing efforts. Unfortunately, if one of your larger Martech tools has an outage, it may be unfeasible to use an alternative. The communication plan outlines how you will communicate to your customers and stakeholders if necessary. Most of the time, Martech outages affect your internal stakeholders, but it is a good idea to have a plan for customer communication just in case.

Lack of support: Another pervasive issue in the Martech industry is the lack of customer support. This takes two forms: the lack of help troubleshooting issues and lack of guidance on projects. Some Martech platforms have so many users that it is difficult to get in contact with support agents without paying a premium fee. In this case, it is a good idea to become familiar with the online help resources and peer community that the vendor has. If there aren't any helpful resources like this, it might be time to switch vendors. Lack of guidance is also a challenge, as many marketers will regularly have new projects and use cases for the platform. Data integrations are also a common one, and without clear guidance and documentation from support, this can be a challenge. The very best solution is to address many of these issues upfront—whether it be contractually or simply to learn how to best get support—however, if you are stuck in a difficult position, you can also turn to consultants and agencies for guidance.

Ideas for a Low-Cost Martech Stack

Some early-stage companies may require the functionality of Martech tools but lack the budget to acquire them. Here are some ideas to help them along.

Mailchimp: Mailchimp is a low-cost email marketing provider. It is easy to use and easy to get started. Recently, Mailchimp has launched features for landing pages, social media, and marketing automation, covering much of what a marketing team needs to engage their customers. Mailchimp is a solid platform to use as a primary Martech engagement tool and can connect to other tools as well.

Hubspot: At the time of this writing, Hubspot's suite of marketing services may be one of the most complete, low-cost ways to implement a comprehensive Martech stack at an affordable cost. Some of Hubspot's service plans are free, and they offer tools for CRM, email marketing, marketing automation, content management, and more. One of the fantastic benefits of using Hubspot is their ever-growing list of native integrations and service partners that help marketers augment their marketing usage. With Hubspot's company growth and network of applications, they are a solid choice to begin building a low-cost but effective Martech stack.

Summary

- Effective Martech stack design begins with thinking about high-level business goals and the customer experience.
- Use these overarching principles when designing your Martech stack: the customer journey, benchmarking, simplicity over complexity, and data integration.
- There are different approaches to building a Martech stack: a lean stack, an enterprise stack, and a hybrid approach.
- Select your Martech platforms with great consideration and long-term thinking.

06

The Core Business Systems and Platforms for Every Marketing Team

What are Core Marketing Systems and Platforms?

Core marketing systems and platforms are technologies that marketers struggle to do their jobs without. They tend to use these platforms on a daily or weekly basis because they are a fundamental part of their jobs. Examples of these platforms are customer databases, marketing automation tools, and reporting tools. Notice that these tools support functions that marketers are typically responsible for, regardless of company size and industry. There are three pillars to core marketing platforms: data, frequent customer engagement, and reporting. In terms of data, most core marketing platforms will store most if not all customer records. Marketing is not possible without customer and prospect data, whether that is to send them messages, grab their attention via advertising, or run reports to understand them better. In terms of the frequent engagement of customers, most of marketing's principal functions involve getting messages in front of customers— whether that be a social media post, email newsletter, or eBook. Technology is required to support these engagements, and most core marketing platforms are built around facilitating this type of customer interaction. Finally, we have reporting, and in the seminal words of management consultant Peter Drucker: "What gets measured, gets managed." Marketers need to facilitate and produce reports on their marketing activities, pull data from the various core marketing systems, and use them to demonstrate their effectiveness—as well as improve their marketing decision-making.

Why are Core Marketing Systems Important?

It's advantageous to have many functions combined into core marketing platforms – this provides consistency for resources, data, and employee training. Marketing automation, for example, encompasses landing pages, email campaigns, and lead management in a single platform, eliminating the need for multiple point solutions to accomplish the same thing. One of the core platforms usually serves as the "marketing system of record." A marketing system of record is typically a robust platform that serves as marketing's control tower. It has visibility into marketing data and customer data, and is the often the source of data for marketing reporting. Having one central system makes it easy for a marketing team to collaborate, as well as build expertise to continue optimizing marketing efforts. It also makes it easy to look back historically, review all marketing campaigns in one place, and repurpose campaigns or improve upon future ones. Without core marketing platforms, marketing teams can be severely limited. It can be time-consuming to use many different tools to accomplish similar tasks, and it is difficult to train and monitor users on many different tools.

System of Record versus Source of Truth

While the marketing system of record is a robust technology platform that the marketing team uses to accomplish many of their tasks, the "source of truth" for a marketing team (and the rest of the go-to-market function) is a database used for historical accuracy. For example, if a sales and marketing team want to be definitive about the source of a lead, which marketing campaigns influenced an opportunity, or which salesperson closed a deal, they would look to the platform that is designated as the source of truth. The platform which is generally driven by a large database that serves as the source of truth often comes up in reporting requirements. Business leaders want confidence in where their data comes from, so having a database that everyone looks to as the source of truth is important. This is also important when it comes to attribution reporting, which means assigning credit for sales to different areas of contribution. In addition, a source of truth database can also be helpful in customer success initiatives, as it may be helpful for an account manager to review this history of contacts within an account and the different issues that have happened in the past. While the marketing system of record and the source of truth are typically different systems, it is possible for them to be the same platform.

When Do Core Marketing Systems Differ?

The core marketing systems tend to stay same regardless of industry and company size. The main variances are in the specific company or vendor for each platform. For example, small businesses may use simple, cost-effective core marketing systems while enterprise companies will use robust, higher-ticket platforms. You may see some differences in a given industry or category based on need, and some of the core platforms may be combined or split out into specific functions. One of the key differences that we have been seeing is based on the volume of data that the company must analyze and action. Companies that have a large number of customers have increased data needs, and would therefore be more likely to purchase a CDP or data warehouse. These companies tend to be larger, and they are able to hire the technical expertise required to manage these platforms. Companies without as many customers can get away with managing data in another platform, such as a CRM, MAP, or proprietary database. There are also cases where Martech providers offer robust core platforms that support multiple functions that typically are supported by separate core platforms. This can make the core part of the tech stack look very different. One final note about core platforms is that there is a steep level of effort required to change to a different vendor. The implementation of a core platform can often take months, and once complete, these platforms house very important and sensitive business data. A platform migration can be quite the undertaking, and it is all the more reason to be very thoughtful when purchasing a core platform.

The Core Systems for B2B versus B2C

Because there are marked differences between B2B marketing and B2C marketing, the core marketing platforms may look a little different (Figure 6.1).

While the B2B core platforms may look like this:

- content management system (CMS);
- customer relationship management (CRM);
- marketing automation platform (MAP);
- customer data platform (CDP);
- analytics platform;
- project management platform.

The B2C platforms may look like this:

- content management system (CMS) + e-commerce marketing;
- customer relationship management (CRM);
- email service provider (ESP);
- data management platform (DMP);
- analytics platform;
- project management platform.

FIGURE 6.1 Core Martech Platforms

FIGURE 6.2 Results of a LinkedIn Poll

What is at the center of your Martech stack today?
You can see how people vote. **Learn more**

CRM	40%
Marketing Automation Platform	38%
Customer Data Platform	15%
Data Warehouse/Data Lake ✅	7%

918 votes · Poll closed · **Remove vote**

Notice that the first difference is that in B2C the CMS is expanded to include e-commerce functionality, since more purchases will likely happen online via website in comparison to B2B. Also, we can see that the MAP is replaced with an ESP. Since lead management and some other core functions that MAP has aren't as necessary in B2C, a platform that focuses on email customization and large deployments is a better fit. Finally, instead of a CDP we see a DMP, which aggregates large amounts of audience and advertising data in one place—since B2C typically does larger advertising campaigns to more consumers.

In a LinkedIn poll of 918 marketers, 40 percent of respondents said that the customer relationship management system (CRM) is at the center of their Martech stack, while 38 percent said the marketing automation platform (MAP) was at the center (Figure 6.2).

Common Core Marketing Platforms

Content Management System (CMS)

What is it? It's almost impossible to talk about Martech without the content management system. A CMS has been defined as, "software that helps users create, manage, and modify content on a website without that need for specialized technical knowledge. In simpler language, a CMS is a tool that helps you build a website without needing to write all the code from scratch." (Sitecore.com) As the company grows and number of marketing campaigns and assets increases, the CMS can become very large.

Why is it a core marketing system? The CMS is a core marketing system because marketing teams use it as the primary engagement mechanism for prospects and customers. The website is the digital storefront of a business, and its look, content, functionality, and offerings define much of how business is done today. Marketing teams spend much time and resources on designing the website, uploading content, building out product marketing, and creating various content experiences for customers to build relationships with their brand.

How do you select a CMS? When evaluating CMS vendors, you should think about functionality, usability, expansion potential, and talent. From a functionality perspective, what features do you need your website to have? Will it be a content-driven site, or will it be an e-commerce store? Will you have hundreds of blog posts, or will you have just a handful of product content pages? It's important to keep these things in mind when picking. The other function you are looking for is customization and what you are looking to do. Some CMS providers only have standard templates that you can customize; if you are looking for something unique or bespoke, you may need a CMS that offers more customization options.

Next you want to think of usability, and this goes hand-in-hand with the skill level of your team. If there isn't much digital proficiency on your team and you won't be bringing on outside help, you will need a CMS that is completely low-code or no-code, meaning that no HTML or CSS experience is required to publish your marketing content. If you have a high level of digital expertise available, then you can look at CMS platforms are more technically sophisticated.

Expansion potential is also important, and this refers to additional functionality and scale that you are looking to add in the future. Websites today can be entirely personalized for each visitor and can offer up truly interactive experiences. If this is something you are looking to do, you should look at CMS platforms that offer many plug-ins, expansions, and add-ons that support this type of experience.

Finally, from a personal perspective, it is also good to look at how you want your skills and the skills of your team to progress in the future. From a career point of view, it is advantageous to learn how to use some of the most popular CMS platforms so that in the future you can list them on your resume—it will contribute to the growth of your career and make you very hirable.

Customer Relationship Management (CRM)

What is it? A customer relationship management system is what a company uses to improve the interactions and connections with buyers and potential buyers, and is typically leveraged by the go-to-market team (sales, marketing, customer success) to track and optimize revenue generation efforts. CRM can be described as "a process in which a business or other organization administers its interactions with customers, typically using data analysis to study large amounts of information. CRM systems compile data from a range of communication channels and allow businesses to learn more about their target audiences and how to best cater for their needs." (Techtarget.com)

While CRM is the process, a CRM system is a platform that manages the process. In marketing, the platform is typically referred to as CRM. One of the particularly useful features of CRM is "deal management." Especially in B2B, sales are a complex process, with many buying members and moving parts. It's important to manage the discovery, evaluation, consideration—and ultimately purchase—in a deal, and this is done digitally through the CRM by managing and tracking the interactions that take place in a deal.

Why is it a core marketing system? The entire go-to-market team leverages the CRM on a daily basis to manage customers, the deal flow, future deals, and the pipeline. Sales inputs interaction data such as calls and meeting notes, and marketing captures behavioral data—such as which campaigns prospects and customers participated in. Because of all this, the CRM often has the most customer data out of all the tools in a tech stack, second only to CDPs and data warehouses. The customer data supports revenue-driving efforts and business reporting. Revenue-efforts are all the initiatives that go-to-market teams engage in to drive sales, whether that be from new customers or existing customers. Business reporting refers to compiling data and organizing it in a way that the leadership can understand what customers are doing and what is driving revenue—improving business decisions in the future. Many marketing initiatives start (or at least layer) in the data from the CRM.

HOW DO YOU SELECT A CRM?

There are many factors you need to consider when selecting a CRM service.

On-premises versus cloud: CRM platforms can either be hosted on-premises or in the cloud. On-premise CRM refers to software services that are hosted locally at a client's location. With the technological advancements of cloud computing, there is very little reason today to go with on-premise CRM. CRM on the cloud offers the benefits of automated backups, global access, and real-time scalability. While some may argue that on-premises CRM may be slightly more secure, the benefits of cloud CRM far outweigh the risks.

Budget: Most of today's CRM providers offer incremental pricing based on users or usage, so budget is typically not as much of an issue as it was in the past. However, micro-businesses or bootstrapped startups that are watching expenses very closely may want to select one of the free or very low-cost options.

Usability and adoption: A CRM is only as good as its adoption rate. When evaluating a CRM vendor, put yourself in the shoes of salespeople, account manager, marketers etc. Will they be able to accomplish their jobs in an efficient and effective way? Is the CRM easy to understand and interact with? In addition to the day-to-day inputting and managing of customer information, the next key functionality of the CRM is reporting. Much of the leads, accounts, pipeline, and revenue information is managed and reported into finance using CRM reports and dashboards. When evaluating a CRM option, make sure to verify that the reports and dashboards display the data you need and in a format that you can use. One framework you can use is to list out the different teams in a matrix, with features listed in the rows, and "need," "want," and "don't need" in the columns. This way you can easily identify which CRM features and functions are critical, nice to have, and not important.

Customization: While CRMs support the basic functions of tracking customer relationships and reporting, many businesses require customizations for their unique needs. The customizations typically come in the form of workflows, custom objects, and integration with other technology. Workflows in CRMS are automated actions that occur based on events and specific criteria. For example, when a lead is entered into a CRM, a workflow could assign the lead to a particular sales rep and send that rep an email alert. Investigate the workflow functionality of each CRM vendor to make sure it will support your needs. Custom objects are also important to many companies, as they allows businesses to augment their database of customer records. An object in a database is like a table or spreadsheet; for example you could have an object of leads, with each row being a person and the columns being information about that person such as name, phone number, and email address. The default objects in CRM are usually leads, contacts, accounts, and opportunities/deals. But let's say a company wants to keep track of specific products a contact purchases, which may not fit into the existing objects. This calls for a custom object, one that tracks purchases, which can easily be cross-referenced with the existing objects. Take a look at the data you have and see if custom objects will be important now or in the future.

Scalability and future potential: It's not just important to think about the needs of your team now, but also in the years to come. Two key things to think about for the future use of your CRM is integration-capability and app marketplaces. As discussed in previous chapters, the ability for data to flow seamlessly across your tech stack is paramount to Martech success. Your CRM should be built with open APIs that make it easy to connect to other platforms. At minimum, check to see if the Martech you are planning on using today integrates with the CRM. As we discussed in earlier chapters, an app marketplace is a collection of partner software that has built-in integrations with the vendor in question. For example, AppExchange (owned by Salesforce) is a directory of thousands of software tools that connect to Salesforce for a variety of use cases. While the CRM you choose may not need thousands of connecting partners, it is important to pick a CRM that has a history of connecting to adjacent applications.

Industry-specific: If your business is similar to many other businesses in a specific industry, it may be worth selecting a CRM that is custom-built for that industry. This can save you the time of ensuring a CRM has the appropriate customizations you need. For example, MindBody is a company that provides a CRM platform—among other tools—to businesses in the health and wellness industry, such as gyms, massage spas, nail salons, and more. Their platform caters to businesses with many members and quick, recurring transactions. Clinico provides a CRM platform dedicated to hospitals and clinics, enabling these businesses to track sensitive patient information and deploy appointment reminders and other communications to patients. If an industry-specific platform is right for you, it may save you a lot of time and energy in CRM customizations.

Marketing Automation Platform (MAP)

The marketing automation platform is sometimes thought of as the marketing system of record because of its robust feature-set and connection into the CRM and other core business systems. Selecting the right MAP for your business is important for your long-term marketing success.

What is it? A MAP programmatically executes many of the promotional and revenue-generating activities for a business. The most popular features in a MAP are email marketing, lead nurturing, lead management, landing pages, lead scoring, personalization, and reporting.

Why is it a core marketing system? MAPs are core marketing systems because they support the management of the main digital touchpoints for customers. Customers engage with businesses across their website, email, paid media, and social media—many of which can be facilitated by marketing automation. To give a real example, let's say you create an industry report and promote it across different digital channels. The conversion point of the campaign will be a landing page and a confirmation email, which will be hosted and sent through the MAP. Regardless of which channel leads come from, the end point will be the MAP. Marketers therefore allocate much of their campaign efforts either in or adjacent to a MAP. Another reason why MAPs are core marketing systems is their lead management capabilities. Leads are an important starting point for marketing to help drive revenue for the business, and making sure leads are being generated and handed off to sales are an important part of marketing. In addition, MAP is a core business system because of its integration with CRM. Many MAPs have a bidirectional sync with a CRM, meaning that the data is the same in both systems. This allows marketing activities to be heavily driven by sales data, and sales activities to be influenced and supported by marketing data. Finally, because marketing automation supports many of the digital customer touchpoints, the MAP is the system that provides much of the data that powers marketing reporting.

How do you select a MAP? Deciding upon a MAP vendor is tricky because there are many to choose from. First, get a sense of your budget and how much of the overall marketing budget you can allocate to a MAP. Enterprise MAPs can easily run close to hundreds of thousands of dollars per year, and if that is out of the question for your team then you can quickly eliminate them. While budget isn't the main factor in MAP selection, you must be realistic in what you can pay.

Next, you want to look at the features, functionality, and usability of the platform. Most MAPs have the same core features such as email marketing and lead management, so much of this comparison will be on the additional features that can add some extra value to your use of the MAP. You also want to keep in mind usability and the talent on your team. Some MAPs are incredibly complex, and it is advisable that you have savvy digital marketing talent your team before attempting to run them. If you feel you don't have the right digital talent on your team, it is advisable to go with a simpler and more straightforward platform. If you feel that you can hire talent internally or externally in the near future, it might be worth purchasing a more robust (albeit harder to learn) platform and growing into it.

Next you want to look at interconnectivity with both existing and future marketing applications. The first is obvious: if your MAP cannot integrate with the existing tools in your stack, you will have difficulty executing marketing in a repeatable, scalable way. Let's say there is no possibility of integrating your webinar platform with your MAP. You will always have incongruent data, and you will always need to export from one platform and import into the other. These manual data updates can cause data inconsistencies and a poor customer experience if there are data errors.

Finally, you want to think about future platform integrations. Create a 3–5-year Martech roadmap (more on that later) and investigate to see if the MAP you are thinking of going with will integrate seamlessly. A lack of integration capability will severely limit your functionality in the future, and will impact your ability to build the robust tech stack that you want.

Customer Data Platform (CDP)

What is it? A customer data platform, usually called a CDP, can be described as "a marketer-managed system designed to collect customer data from all sources, normalize it and build unique, unified profiles of each individual customer. The result is a persistent, unified customer database that shares data with other marketing systems." A CDP connects with other platforms in a tech stack and aggregates data in once place. Data normalization and standardization is an important part of the CDP, since data can be in different formats in different systems. Once a single, unified view of a customer is created, marketers can better understand what drives customer behavior and act on those insights.

Why is it a core marketing system? "Data" should probably give you a big clue as to why a CDP is a core system. The truth is that there are many benefits from getting a unified view of the customer. The first is insights. If marketers can see how customers became aware of their brand, if/how they converted, and many other aspects of their digital behavior, it can help them to learn about customers and make better decisions on how to market to them.

Second, having all of the data from different systems in one place helps to activate that data and engage customers. A core part of activating data (and engaging customers where they are) is defining a target audience for marketing initiatives. CDPs allow you to combine different customer attributes such as demographic, firmographic, behavior, and product usage into a single place so that you can easily build an audience for marketing campaigns.

CAN WE JUST USE A DATA WAREHOUSE OR MARKETING DATA LAKE INSTEAD?

One option that you could consider instead of a CDP is to use a data warehouse or marketing data lake. Data warehouses and marketing data lakes are storage systems for data that aggregate data from many systems in one place over a period of time. While you can get many of the same benefits out of a data warehouse or marketing data lake that you can get from a CDP, these systems typically require engineering and/or development talent. The benefit of a CDP is that marketing teams can interact and activate their data in real-time, rather than having to wait for more technical talent to do it for them.

How do you select a CDP? Here are the key things you want to think about when selecting a CDP. First is the ability for the CPD to integrate with all of the relevant platforms in your tech stack. You may be using an analytics platform, CRM, MAP, and other systems. Ensure the data can flow from those systems into your CDP seamlessly. Next you want to think about compliance and security. All your customer data will be housed in the CDP, therefore you want to make sure that the vendor stores and protects the data in a compliant and secure way (think GDPR). In addition, you want to consider ease-of-use relative to the level of tech talent on your team. Your team should be able to regularly utilize the CDP to build segments, analyze customer data, and activate the data to engage customers.

Analytics Platform

What is it? Marketing analytics has been described as "a math-based discipline that seeks to find patterns in your marketing strategy to improve your marketing performance. Analytics employs statistics, predictive modeling, and machine learning to reveal insights and answer questions." (Mailchimp.com) In short, an analytics platform is a tool that marketing teams use to understand, dissect, and report on their marketing initiatives. For example, all the campaign data, website data, and marketing-generated revenue data would flow into the analytics platform where marketers would run reports. This is different to a CDP because marketers use the analytics platform specifically for analytics and reporting, rather than creating a unified view of the customer or for activation.

Why is it a core marketing system? Marketing analytics really comes down to two questions:

1 How is our marketing performing?

2 How will we use our marketing time and budget for the greatest possible return in the future?

Marketing teams need to be able to aggregate their marketing data in one place for deep analysis, and then report those results to leadership and the rest of the organization on a regular basis. Without an analytics platform, marketers are stuck exporting data from multiple systems, and then trying to unify that data in spreadsheets or other manual means. This can be time-consuming and potentially fraught with error. Since analytics and reporting are foundational to good marketing, a dependable analytics platform is a core marketing system.

WHAT ARE THE FOUR TYPES OF ANALYTICS?

There are four types of analytics, and it is important to understand each one and when to use them. The first is descriptive analytics, which answers the question "what happened?" This involves looking at past data to see what has occurred, whether it is an increase or decrease in sales, traffic, and/or conversions etc. Next is diagnostic analytics, which answers the question, "why did it happen?" Once you have determined an event, diagnostic analytics looks at the possible causes and reasons for it happening. Third is predictive analytics, which answers the question "what is likely to occur in the future?" You do this by looking at historical data and trends, and making smart predictions about what results you can expect in the future. Lastly there is prescriptive analytics, which tries to answer the question "what should be done?" Remember that the end goal of marketing analytics is to figure out where to invest for the highest possible marketing return. By reviewing the first three types of analytics, you can make better decisions on where to spend your marketing dollars.

MARKETING ATTRIBUTION

A hot topic in marketing today is marketing attribution, which is the practice of assigning revenue credit to marketing campaigns or marketing initiatives to evaluate effectiveness. This is not to be confused with marketing ROI, which is a formula calculation that outputs a percentage, letting you know if you made good on a marketing investment. Marketing attribution tells you which campaigns were most effective, so you can make decisions to optimize your marketing efforts. The key thing is to understand the different types of marketing attribution, when to use each one, and their limitations. The first is single-touch attribution, which consists of first-touch and last-touch. First-touch attribution gives all of the marketing credit to the campaign that first engaged a lead—and was typically how the lead became known to our Martech ecosystem. Last-touch attribution gives all the credit to the campaign that last engaged a prospect before they were converted into an opportunity/deal, which is typically one of the last stages in a lead lifecycle. While single-touch attribution gives you valuable insights into which of your campaigns are doing what, the common opposition to single-touch is that it doesn't tell the whole story. Multi-touch attribution gives credit to multiple campaigns that engaged a customer during their journey. There are different types such as linear and weighted multi-touch attribution. Linear multi-touch attribution gives credit equally to every single campaign that touched the customer before they converted into an opportunity/deal. Weighted multi-touch attribution gives a different percentage of credit based on where the touchpoint occurred. For example, you may weight the first-touch or last-touch higher than engagements that happened in the middle of the journey. The important thing to remember is that attribution is meant to give you information so you can make better decisions—it's not an indicator of what is right or wrong. Finally, keep in mind that marketing attribution today fails to account for the touchpoints that marketing systems have difficulty tracking, such as word of mouth, social media mentions, and referrals, so even if you put together a robust attribution model, you still will not get the full picture.

How do you select an analytics platform? Similar to selecting other core Martech platforms, you want to check for integrations and usability. Your analytics platform must be able to connect with the different pieces of engagement technology you have such as marketing automation and advertising platforms, as well as platforms that hold your customer data, such as CRM and CDP. From a usability standpoint, you want to consider dashboarding, granular analysis, and shareability. For dashboarding, your team should be able to format the layout of your dashboards and reports in a clear, understandable way that gives you the information you need. Next is granular analysis. You want your analytics platform to be able to slice and dice data in a way that allows you to understand the efficacy of your marketing programs and how it contributes to business results. For example, you should be able to compare which the investment in campaigns, which campaigns are good at driving new customers versus expanding existing ones, and how much ROI you can expect from your marketing budget. The next is shareability, specifically having the reports and data be accessible to the various stakeholders that may need to view it. Some platforms may not allow you to have many users, and it can be cumbersome to have to export the data and/or take screenshots and share them with the team. Ask about "view-only" user capability, where it will be free or low-cost to add users who will not necessarily be able to utilize all aspects of the analytics platform, but can view the reports and make minor customizations—such as the date range.

Options for Limited Resources

The main constraints you will see in regard to picking the right analytics platform for your team is limited budget and lack of technical talent. Analytics platforms unfortunately can be on the expensive side, and while some platforms are easy to use, most analytics platforms do require a reasonable level of digital savvy. If you can't commit to an analytics platform for these reasons, you first want to turn to your CRM. The reporting and dashboarding capabilities of many of the leading CRMs can combine sales and marketing data in an effective way, and can offer up basic analytics features. The last option—and definitely nothing to be ashamed of—is to download the data from all different platforms and organize it in a spreadsheet, such as Google Sheets or Microsoft Excel. While not very scalable, the benefit to reporting on spreadsheets is that you can manipulate the data exactly the way you want, without technology or talent requirements. Many experts recommend that marketers create reports in Excel as a first step to getting the fundamentals right, before moving on to a more advanced platform.

Project and Workflow Management

What is it? A project management or workflow management tool helps teams plan, manage, report on, and optimize projects of all sizes. Typically, a project management tool offers multiple seats where each member of a project team can log on, view the goals and timeline of a platform, and work on tasks and assign tasks to other members. Some project management tools offer customizable work-flows, which automate some of the manual tasks project managers typically have to do themselves.

Why is it a core marketing system? Some may be surprised that project and workflow management is considered a core marketing technology; however, without project management, marketing cannot be implemented. Everything from publishing a blog article to a plat-form migration can be considered a project, and projects with multiple collaborators and stakeholders become increasingly difficult to manage. In an efficient marketing team, the project management software hosts the majority of initiatives marketers work on, and where they will spend a majority of their time.

How do you select a project management platform? Aside from an organization's budget and the features required, project management platform selection depends heavily on stakeholder preference. Once you've narrowed down the platforms to a shortlist based on how much you can afford and the features you need, you want to test drive each tool. Ideally, you will be able to get feedback from multiple stakeholders. Have as many future users as possible participate in a pilot or free trial, and try to run a small project through the platform. Then answer these questions: Were we able to plan and hit key mile-stones? Were we able to collaborate on tasks? How was communication through the platform? Are we happy with the post-project reports? Once you've completed the pilot, select the platform that performed best for your specific team's needs.

The Value in Picking Industry-Leading Solutions

One of the key factors worth highlighting when it comes to vendor selection is the value in choosing industry-leading solutions. An industry-leading solution is a platform/vendor that has been around longer than most of its competitors, is typically larger than the competition, and is consistently rated higher by analysts and review sites. While industry leaders may not work for every company and can certainly be more expensive, there are some key benefits to picking them over others.

Proven long-term potential: The Martech landscape is rapidly changing, with new entrants coming in and existing providers closing shop seemingly every day. With this volatility, it is worth it to consider selecting vendors that have proven themselves as a viable business service to many businesses over a long period of time. These larger vendors usually work with many types of companies across industries with a multitude of use cases—these proven case studies can lend much confidence, especially if your marketing hinges on getting this service up and running.

More resources: Industry leaders will typically have more resources than their smaller competitors. This includes more support staff, technical resources, training and technical documentation, and integration resources. If your team has never implemented a certain type of software before, these resources can make the difference between success and failure.

Peer networks/communities: When it comes to Martech, never underestimate the value of a community. Leading vendors, especially those that have been around for a while, will have large user bases that can serve to be a helpful resource. Some vendors have vibrant communities—online and offline—of peers who can help you with your questions or can even serve as a future talent pool.

Portfolio of services: Some industry leaders, especially the large tech companies like Salesforce, Adobe, Microsoft, and Oracle, offer many different Martech services under a single umbrella. While these services may not be included in a single platform, many offer the ability to pay on one purchase order and to work with the same customer success team. This type of alignment can be valuable if you are looking to onboard many tools very quickly and can minimize the procurement effort. Additionally, it's common for all the tools within a vendor's portfolio to integrate together seamlessly, so worrying about connecting the platforms together won't be a problem. Note, however, that just because one of the vendor's platforms may be an industry-leading platform, it doesn't mean that all of them are. Make sure to go through the features and benefits analysis with each tool under a portfolio company's umbrella.

Summary

- Core marketing systems are Martech that every business should have as the center of their tech stack.
- The core marketing systems are typically: CRM, MAP, CDP, analytics, and project management.
- There is additional value is selecting industry-leading solutions for your core marketing systems.

07

Identifying Value-Add Marketing Platforms and Tools

Now that you have the core Martech platforms in place, it's time to start adding ancillary tools to your stack. But you can't take a lackadaisical approach to purchasing tools—it's important to add Martech strategically. Here is what you need to know when adding more Martech tools to your stack.

According to a LinkedIn poll I ran of 679 marketers, 51 percent say that after core tools, they would add a reporting and analytics platform, followed by 26 percent of marketers who say they would add a data enrichment platform (Figure 7.1).

This is a great indicator of what is considered important in terms of additional tools for marketers today. Let's take a look at the principles of adding Martech (see Figure 7.2).

Overarching Principles in Adding Martech

Goals

One of the key concepts in life and work is to "begin with the end in mind," which is borrowed from Stephen Covey's *The 7 Habits of Highly Effective People* (Covey, 2007). The technology in your tech stack should be intentional, and each should move you towards your marketing goals in some way. One way to look at this is in terms of inputs and outputs. An input is an activity that your marketing team

FIGURE 7.1 Results of a LinkedIn Poll

Your company already has a CRM, Marketing Automation, Content Management System, & Customer Data Platform. Your next Martech purchase is...?

You can see how people vote. **Learn more**

Data Enrichment	**26%**
Webinar Platform	**7%**
Reporting/Analytics Tools	**51%**
Project Management ✓	**17%**

679 votes • Poll closed • **Remove vote**

FIGURE 7.2 Martech Selection

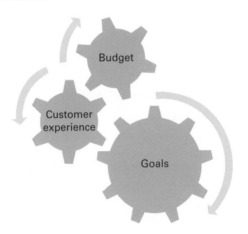

creates or performs, while an output is a high-value action that customer takes. A simple example is promoting an educational event where you invite customers and prospects. The inputs are the campaigns that you deploy to promote the event, which could be paid advertising, social media posts, and email invitations. The outputs are the action that your prospects and customers take, which, in this case, is registering and attending the event. You must have determined with your team beforehand the key outputs that indicate that you are on track to achieve your goal (in this case, registrations and attendance), and then consider the marketing tools that you will need to increase the outputs. While you can and should subscribe to tools that allow you to increase the volume and quality of inputs, always remember that outputs are more important as they lead to business outcomes that help your team achieve their goals.

Customer Experience (CX)

A primary objective of Martech is to improve the customer experience. At Amazon for example, this concept is referred to as "customer obsession." Much of Amazon's success can be attributed to thinking about all their decisions through a customer-first mentality. Giving customers the best experience, whether it be through product, service, or engagement, puts your company ahead of the competition. For marketing, the customer experience is all touchpoints where customers engage with your company. This is a company's advertising, website, digital channels, sales and customer service and more. Two questions that help improve customer experience is ask "are customers getting what they want from this touchpoint?" And "how can we deliver the experience of that touchpoint in a more delightful way?" For example, when thinking about a website page or landing page that promotes a digital report to your audience, ask these questions:

- Can the visitor to this landing page quickly ascertain what this report is about and why they should read it?
- Does the page and all images load quickly?
- Can the visitor get access to the report easily, or are there multiple hurdles that hinder them (excessive form length, multiple steps to access report, etc.)?
- Does the visitor feel that they can trust your company, especially when it comes to their data?

These questions are just a starting point. Continue to identify ways to make the touchpoint experience more delightful for customers and ensure you have the right marketing platforms to support it.

Budget

In a LinkedIn poll of 487 marketers, 60 percent of respondents said that advertising and promotion tools take up the majority of the Martech budget (Figure 7.3).

When it comes to purchasing Martech, your budget will be highly situational. Generally speaking, your spend on Martech should make up approximately 10–20 percent of your overall marketing budget for the year. This may be significantly higher if you work in a tech-related industry or other progressive sector. For the sake of this example, let's assume your Martech budget is 20 percent of your annual marketing budget. The first 10–15 percent of that portion of the budget should be allocated to your core marketing platforms. This means that you will be working with approximately 5–10 percent of your annual marketing budget to purchase additional marketing tools. Depending on your company, this may narrow down the options of vendors to a shortlist of tools that fits your budget. This does not mean that any tool outside your budget is completely off limits. If you have identified a marketing platform that will generate ROI for the business, you can perform ROI calculations and write up a business case that justifies this purchase to leadership and finance. You can position ROI as revenue-generated, pipeline-generated, time-saved, or productivity-gained—as well as other outcomes that could result from using the new tool.

FIGURE 7.3 Results of a LinkedIn Poll

Which of these Martech categories do you think takes the most of the Martech budget?

You can see how people vote. **Learn more**

Advertising and Promotion	**60%**
Commerce and Sales	**11%**
Content and Experience	**24%**
Social and Relationships ✓	**5%**

487 votes · Poll closed · **Remove vote**

Identifying Additional Needs

Now that we've covered the high-level principles of selecting value-added tools for your Martech stack, it's time to get tactical to understand the actual process of building out your Martech stack. Selecting additional tools is a great time to gain competitive advantage and really make your marketing goals a reality.

When I was working for a mid-sized enterprise a few years ago, I found that we had a pervasive data-quality problem. The leads in our CRM had information that was missing or outdated, and the sales team were constantly complaining about not having the account information they needed to properly engage prospects. After conducting online research and speaking with a few peers, I found that a data enrichment platform could help us address these issues. After evaluating a shortlist of vendors, I purchased and implemented the new data enrichment platform, and saw an immediate benefit to the sales process and other data-related processes.

Sometimes adding additional Martech is as easy as that scenario; other times it will be much harder to find what you need. Here are key points to consider when trying to identify additional need for Martech.

Conduct a simplified gap analysis: One of the best methods to identify additional Martech is a gap analysis. A gap analysis is when you take inventory of all of your existing technology and then find any holes or "gaps" that are missing based on the functionality that you need. While a full gap analysis can be a useful tool, I find it more practical and effective to do a simplified version of a gap analysis. The first step is to list out a process to achieve an objective. For example, if your objective is to convert a lead into a sale, your process will be to attract the attention of a prospective buyer, engage the prospect to spend time reviewing your company, set a meeting with the prospect to sell your services, and finally get the prospect to sign a purchase order. Now for each of these steps, think about the optimal experience for the prospect or customers, and determine if you have the right technology to create that experience.

For example, if you want to attract a customer's attention with a helpful/educational content video, do you have the tools to create, edit, and publish the video? How about to socialize the video on different platforms? In terms of engagement, do you have the tools you need to deliver an opportunity via pop-up or chatbot that allows a prospect to enter their information? For setting up a meeting, would it be easier if the prospect could select a time themselves to speak with the first available salesperson? By thinking of a gap analysis this way, you can allow your strategy and outcomes to drive the technology you use, rather than the other way around.

Conduct stakeholder surveys: While it is helpful to do self-planning, remember that you are not the only one who is trying to drive business objectives, and you are not the only one engaging customers. Stakeholder alignment is key to success in Martech, and to a cohesive marketing strategy that gets adopted. One of the best ways to get quick feedback from many stakeholders is surveys. If needed, there are cost-effective ways to conduct internal surveys, such as using SurveyMonkey or Google Forms. Depending on your company, your internal Martech survey may look very different. However, here are some questions to get you started:

- Do you have the tools you need to effectively perform your role? If not, what are you missing?

- What parts of your role do you have challenges with? Are there any particular technology challenges?

- How is your experience engaging with customers? What are the pain points?

- What tools and processes do you use to do your job? Are there processes that take too long or are redundant?

- What is the most frustrating technology process involved in your role?

- If you could improve the customer experience with technology, what would you do?

These are great starter questions. Once you have answers to these questions, keep in mind you can also simply email stakeholders these questions and ask for responses, organize the responses by category and function, and determine which problems can be made better through purchasing additional Martech.

Talking to Martech Agencies and Subject Matter Experts

Another method to procuring good intel on additional tools that can help your team achieve their marketing goals is to learn from Martech agencies and other subject matter experts. Martech agencies service a wide variety of clients, usually businesses of different sizes and industries. In addition, these clients have a plethora of challenges and budgets to deal with them; so naturally these agencies can give intelligent recommendations based on particular situations. However, take caution and remember that Martech agencies will try to onboard you as a client, since that is their primary source of business. While this doesn't mean that you should not talk to agencies, keep in mind that you should not ask them to work for free.

Subject matter experts (SMEs) are another invaluable resource, and they may come in the form of independent consultants, authors, former Martech leaders and more. A one-on-one meeting with an SME can uncover great insights. Similar to Martech agencies, subject matter experts have worked on a variety of projects across the space, and can give you some candid advice, whereas an agency may shy away from giving you actionable intel if it doesn't serve their interests.

Here are questions to ask Martech agencies and subject matter experts:

- What marketing technology has been effective for companies of my size and industry?
- What have your clients been using to solve [challenge]?
- What are some downsides of [tool/technology]?
- What are key things we need to think about before working with [vendor]?

- What are some great tools that integrate with [tool]?
- How do you help your clients solve [challenge]?

How Do You Judge the Quality of a Martech Agency?

There are a multitude of Martech agencies out there. I've worked with many agencies of varying quality, and can tell you that selecting the right agency can make a significant difference in your business. But how can you tell if an agency is good or bad? Here are three recommendations.

Comprehension: When you work with a Martech agency, you should understand what problems they are trying to solve and how they intend to help *you* solve it. One of the biggest problems in marketing technology is the concept of the "black box." The black box refers to any technology, solution, or process where it is unclear how it works and how it can be improved or replicated. Some agencies love keeping solutions in this metaphorical black box, because it keeps clients dependent on them. Since clients do not understand what the agency is doing or how they are providing value, it becomes difficult to terminate their contract. In some cases, it also becomes difficult to launch any new technology project without consulting the agency first. Needless to say, a good agency will not hide their solutions in a black box. When you work with a first-rate agency, you will understand the problems you are facing better, and you will understand how they will use their expertise and resources to help you. A good agency relationship will be based on trust, authority, and expertise.

Proven results: You should be working with an agency that can articulate the work they have done in the past with their portfolio of clients, and can walk you through step-by-step how they created value. While not a deal breaker, it's a good idea to work with agencies that have helped companies similar to yours in size and industry—and an even better idea to ask for references. A bad agency will have trouble retaining clients, and you will be hard pressed to find a previous client that will speak highly of them.

Identifying solutions versus problems: You want to make sure you are working with an agency that will bring forward tenable solutions and help you deliver them; versus constantly finding more problems within your business. While it's true that problem identification is part of an agency's role, watch out for bad agencies that will constantly seek ways to charge more for their work. For example, while an agency is commissioned to help with a particular project, they may start reaching into different areas of the business and proposing additional work for them to do. This may be appropriate in some scenarios, ideally infrequently, but remember that an agency should focus on their main responsibility. Agencies that spend more time trying to get more money out of a client rather than solving problems are dangerous to work with.

Colleagues and Review Sites

One of the best methods to obtain candid opinions and recommendations is to talk with colleagues and to check out review sites. Most of the time, your colleagues in similar roles at different companies will be objective third-parties that you can speak with to get the full scoop on Martech that can help you achieve your objectives. Compared to agencies and vendors, colleagues don't have a business interest in recommending solutions to you. Connect with other marketing professionals on LinkedIn and other platforms and set up in-person or virtual coffee chats. Ask them how they solved particular business problems, and if they like certain Martech platforms. In exchange, you can share your experience and make recommendations that they may not have heard of.

Technology reviews sites are also a valuable resource. These sites crowdsource ratings and reviews of different marketing technology, and are a quick way to get multiple opinions on a specific tool. After doing vendor comparisons on these sites, make sure to pay it forward by reviewing the tools that you use and help future marketers with their technology research.

FIGURE 7.4 Results of a LinkedIn Poll

For marketers—what is your role in purchasing a new Martech tool or platform?

You can see how people vote. **Learn more**

I am a key decision-maker ✅	41%
I am key influencer	35%
I'm consulted for my opinion	13%
I find out afterwards	12%

474 votes • Poll closed • **Remove vote**

How Do You Select the Right Vendor?

In a LinkedIn poll of 474 marketers, 41 percent said they were the decision-maker for Martech purchases, while 35 percent said they were a key influencer in the buying decision (Figure 7.4).

Once you have identified the need for particular category of Martech, how do you go about selecting the best vendor for your business? There are many high-level principles to keep in mind when comparing and ultimately choosing a Martech provider.

Budget and Shortlist

By doing the calculations and revenue potential analysis that we discussed earlier, you should easily be able to find multiple vendors that will fit your need as well as your budget. While budget shouldn't be the primary factor in deciding which vendor you go with, we have to be realistic in not choosing vendors that we could never afford. After researching and contacting vendors for pricing, you should be left with a shortlist of Martech providers to choose from.

Hierarchy of Decisions

One excellent way of comparing Martech vendors and ultimately deciding upon a tool for your team is to go through a hierarchy of decisions. Going through each of these steps will put you on the right track to selecting the vendor that is right for you. The first of these is comparing "needs to have," which means cutting out any of the vendors that do not provide a critical feature that you have decided is non-negotiable. Let's say, for example, that you are choosing between webinar providers. You have decided that integration with your specific MAP is non-negotiable. Three out of four of the vendors integrate with your MAP, but the fourth webinar vendor doesn't. This makes it an easy option to eliminate. In some scenarios, this may whittle down your list so much that deciding becomes much easier. In other cases, all of the vendors may meet your critical needs.

Next you want to compare the "nice to have" feature set. These are features that you have decided are not critical to your needs but would provide benefit if you had them. There may only be one or two vendors that have more "nice to have" features than the rest, helping you to eliminate more vendors from the list.

Finally, if the first two evaluation steps are complete and you still have multiple options, you want to make a decision based on usability and preference. To do this, you and other key users should test out the different providers in the form of a trial or pilot. Consider these questions: Which tool is easier to learn? Which tool is easier to navigate? Which tool fits your overall team better? While these questions are subjective in nature, since you have gone through all of the more technical comparisons, all that is left to do is pick a favorite, which will ultimately lead to more adoption and usage in the future.

Key Vendor Evaluation Questions

Especially for higher-ticket Martech platforms, it will be common to meet with the sales team of the vendor to learn about pricing, features, and other important service information. Even if you do not meet with the sales team and opt for online-only research, make sure you ascertain answers to these key questions before you make a purchase decision.

Can this tool support our current lead and data structure? Most marketing technology helps engage or generate leads in some fashion, and it is important that the new tool will work with your overarching lead lifecycle. If the new tool is generating leads, make sure it can tag/update the leads with the correct information, such as lead source and UTM parameters so you can track your efforts. In addition, ensure the new tool delivers data to your other systems in a usable format, otherwise you will be stuck with a ton of manual effort.

What does data security and compliance look like for the new tool? One key component that often goes overlooked is data security and compliance. Data security refers to how your data and your customers' data is stored and protected in the Martech tool in question. Vendors that do not take steps to properly secure your data can be exposed to malicious threats, and you could lose your data or have your customers' data compromised. If this happens, it is a huge breach of trust for your customers and could have long-term consequences for your business. In addition, you want to ask if the vendor stores and uses data in a compliant way. For example, GDPR requires expressed consent (users explicitly opt-in via a checkbox) in many data collection scenarios, and also requires that companies remove customer data if requested. Not following these regulations could result in hefty fines, for both the vendor and anyone using the vendor's services.

How can we receive support? What if the service goes down? While this may seem like a basic question, you would be surprised by how many technology vendors do not provide support to paying customers by default. Make sure to find out if there is any support available at all if you encounter technical issues, and if you have to pay for additional support. Some vendors offer support only to their enterprise customers—meaning the customers that pay them the most. Depending on the type of tool you are considering, customer support may not be a large factor. For example, if you are using a platform to help pick stock images for your website, or for heat map tracking that you occasionally use, it may not make a big difference if you can get support or not, so long as the service eventually works again. But for tools with a high price tag that support a critical marketing function, it's a good idea to have support available and to be able to contact them. You also want to consider what will happen if there is a service outage. Ask how many service outages the vendor has had in the past 12 months, and for how long each outage was. While not as common, you need to make sure their uptime is acceptable, especially in some essential service industries like government and healthcare.

How do price increases work? You should find out what happens when your annual contract comes to an end. Your contract will protect you from any price hikes for the length of your contract, but renewing might be a different story. Some technology vendors include a mandatory 8 percent price increase every year, which will compound over multiple years. While you should technically be realizing more ROI out of a platform every year, percent increases for high-priced services can really add up. Make sure to consider all the possibilities and ramifications if there are mandatory price increases, especially switching costs. Some platforms, such as the core marketing systems, are very hard to switch vendors.

What to Look for in a Demo?

A majority of Martech today is software-as-a-service (SAAS), which means that you will inevitably have to attend software demonstrations, or demos. These are typically conducted by a live salesperson, either on-site at your office or via a virtual screen share. Be cautious— salespeople are great at highlighting the strengths of their platforms, while downplaying the weaknesses. It's our job to seek out any problems, and ensure that this potential platform will work for our needs. Here are key things to keep in mind.

Don't get distracted by pretty interfaces: Many platforms today are cutting-edge, and the user interface (UI) may look modern and elegant. The way a platform looks might be an eye-catching quality, but what we are looking for is a platform that fits our needs. Rather than get distracted by flashy buttons and dashboards, imagine your team working in the platform on a daily basis. How many clicks does it take to accomplish a task? Can you get the data you need? Will all your users have the right permissions and capabilities to perform their jobs? Many sellers will spend a lot of time on the visually appealing parts of their platforms, and spend limited time, if any, on the parts that may not show the platform's best side. Remember that you are not buying a platform for the way it looks, but for the value it provides to your team.

Consider your specific use case: Many sellers will tell you about all the cool things other companies do with their platform, and all the bells and whistles on offer. But remember, you are searching for a tool that will fill a specific need. You need to be able to accomplish an activity or variety of activities repeatedly over time. If the Martech tool cannot achieve certain functions, or requires too great an effort, purchasing the platform will not be worth it. Keep in mind that your team will be using the tool regularly, and you should not let minor features outweigh more important factors in your decision.

Identify weaknesses and problem areas: Unfortunately, most marketers go into software demos and think, "in what ways can I use this platform?" The truth is, there will be other opportunities later to do that. When you go into a demo, you really should be looking for weaknesses and problem areas. Think step-by-step how your team will use the tool and where the problems could come up. Do you have the data in-house to really get ROI out of the tool? Do you have the technical expertise to effectively use the application? How will you know if your use of the tool is generating results or not? All of these are key questions that you should think about during the software demonstration. Make sure to push the salesperson to answer some of your toughest questions in order to get the most value out of the demo.

How to Run a Pilot Program

One of the best ways to evaluate marketing software is to run a pilot program. A pilot program is a low-cost or limited cost trial run of an application where you implement the tool in the field, to be utilized by stakeholders at your company. This is an extremely beneficial method of evaluating software because it takes you out of the realm of theoretical and gives you real feedback as to how the tool will work for your organization. If you are fortunate enough to score a pilot with a software vendor, here are the key steps you need to think about to conduct a successful pilot.

Step 1: Set Pilot Goals

Many organizations make the mistake of starting a pilot program without proper planning and goal setting. Unfortunately, this leads to lack of adoption, and after the pilot you have little sense of the value of the tool for your organization. You should set goals for the pilot program on multiple dimensions. First should be tangible business outcomes. What are the business results you are looking to achieve? Should this technology drive awareness, leads, engagement, conversions, and/or revenue? A good example looks like this: by the end of the pilot program, this technology will have helped us drive 25 percent net new leads compared to the prior time period. You should also set adoption goals for your pilot. This will ensure that your users are utilizing the software in the intended way so you have a valid pilot. Your adoption goal could look like this: over the course of the 60-day pilot, we will have 80 percent or more of the users logging into the platform at least once a week. Keep in mind that this will look different for your organization, try to pick a goal that matches the SMART framework (specific, measurable, actionable, realistic, and time-bound).

Step 2: Get Buy-In

Here's the next big mistake Martech managers make when conducting a pilot: failing to get buy-in from leadership and stakeholders. For a majority of marketing technology, you will need several people and/or teams to learn and use the tool on a regular basis. The problem? Your coworkers are busy, and trying out a new application may be the last thing on their mind. To solve this, you need to meet with them and communicate the value of trying out this pilot. Start with top-level leaders. For example, if you are running a pilot program for the sales team, you should meet with the VP of sales and/or the sales director to communicate the intended outcome for the program, for example: "We think that by testing out this software, we will generate 15 percent more qualified opportunities for sales per month." Now that you have leadership attention, it will be easier to get on the calendar of your intended users. To continue our example, you now have secured the blessing of sales leadership to schedule meetings with the managers and their teams to articulate the importance of the pilot and what you are trying to accomplish. By securing buy-in before running the pilot program, you've greatly increased your chance for success.

Step 3: Host Training

Here is another common mistake Martech managers make when rolling out a pilot: failing to train users on how to use the pilot platform. How can you get a good idea if the software will benefit your organization if no one knows how to use it? Take advantage of the buy-in you received from leadership and set up training sessions with all intended users. Good software vendors will assist with this effort, and will designate a trainer to join a call and help you administer the training. Couple this with training documentation and video recordings and you should be in a good place to launch your pilot.

Step 4: Provide Check-Ins

Don't launch a program and let it run on its own. You should create weekly or biweekly check-in sessions to review how users are doing and identify the challenges they are facing. Many Martech platforms show usage reports, which provide data on what users are doing, such as how many times they are logging in. Use that data in conjunction with email checkups to make sure you are giving this software a fair pilot. Remember that stakeholders are busy, and if no one uses the tool, you won't get much information from the pilot.

Step 5: Set Up a Post-Pilot Debrief

After the pilot is complete, you should set up two post-pilot debrief meetings. The first meeting should be with the vendor, where you will ask for all usage data, results data, and any other information they can provide that will help you make a decision. Next, set up an internal debrief meeting with key stakeholders and leadership to review the results of the pilot. Make sure to address these questions: Did we achieve our goals with the pilot? Why or why not? How was the adoption rate? Did the software work as intended? Do we feel we will realize ROI with this platform if we purchase it? Try to stay as objective as possible (which can be difficult since the pilot required significant effort) when evaluating the results. You also want to make sure that you are inviting key stakeholders to give both quantitative and qualitative feedback about their experience with the software. After reviewing all of these data points from multiple stakeholders, you should have enough information to make a purchasing decision.

Working with Startup Vendors

When looking for Martech providers to serve your needs, you may come across early-stage companies. These startups will be small and scrappy, and may or may not fill the specific need you have for your marketing organization. There are different scenarios which may indicate that it is a good idea to use a startup like this, and other times when it isn't such a great idea.

PROS OF WORKING WITH STARTUP VENDORS

There are several pros to working with startup vendors, including their future roadmap, agility, service, and cost.

One of the great benefits of working closely with startup vendors is the ability to guide their future roadmap. Small startups may not have many customers, and it is common for a founder to hop on a call with customers to find out how it is going. In this case, you may have real influence on their future roadmap, and your dream list of features may soon be a reality.

Startups are also very agile and can deploy fixes and feature enhancements much faster than their enterprise counterparts, who may release new features once a quarter, or even once a year. This comes in real handy when talking about bug fixes—startups can sometimes be very motivated to make customers happy, so the deployment of a patch to fix a recently reported bug may happen very quickly. Some startups also provide an "extra mile" of service because they are trying to prove themselves against their competition. This may mean that they will do things outside the normal scope of your contract to help you out—and may even do pro-bono consulting to make you successful with their platform.

Finally, cost may also be a benefit of working with these smaller startups. Since the number of customers is extremely important to startups (they want to get as many users and as much feedback as possible) you will typically see a lower price point than enterprise software providers.

CONS OF WORKING WITH STARTUPS

While the pros of working with startups are numerous, you should pay equal attention to the cons. The cons of working with startups include security and reliability, outlook, and lack of integrations.

Startups are notorious for moving fast and "breaking things" in order to achieve results, and it is not uncommon that there may be some holes in their code or processes. Data security requires a lot more money and resources than you would expect, and if you are relying on the startup to protect customer-sensitive data, make sure you are comfortable with the level of data security they provide. There are some startups that may not have the technical resources and bandwidth to ensure the uptime that you require. For example, depending on how the startup is hosting its services, you may experience more outages and lag time compared to an enterprise vendor.

Another key thing to be careful of is a startup's outlook. The tech industry has cutthroat competition, and we see new vendors popping up and others closing down every month. While in the short term you probably don't need to be worried that your startup vendor will go out of business, you do need to think cautiously about it over 3–5 years. Ask questions about the startup's funding and growth trajectory and make sure you are comfortable with their level of stability before working with them.

The final con of working with startup companies is their potential lack of integrations and partners. Companies typically focus their deep, native integrations for large-enterprise platforms, and they may not have even heard of the startup vendor that you may be using. While it's not impossible to create custom integrations or find a partner to do it for you, you definitely want to keep that in mind, as moving data between your systems is paramount to Martech success.

Recommendations for Additional Marketing Technology

While the core marketing systems that you use will not vary too much, the additional Martech you purchase can create wide variations. Core marketing systems are a lot like a generic item of clothing—say pants. Within that broad category (an outer garment covering both legs) is limitless variation; from suit-trousers to skinny jeans, zebra-print flares and beyond! In the same way, additional Martech may differ according to the wants and needs of an organization. Here are some wide-ranging recommendations for additional marketing technology.

Webinar/online event provider: This is an important consideration to have in any Martech stack, especially with the growth of digital and the rise of remote work. Many professionals are attending events online, and it is important to create a great online event experience for them. In addition, you can save time and effort by choosing a webinar platform that integrates seamlessly with the other tools in your tech stack, particularly the marketing automation platform. As an example, GoToWebinar integrates with many of the major marketing automation platforms, and automatically syncs attendee data for quick analysis and automated follow-up.

Content experience platform: What is a content experience platform? In short, it's any tool that helps you create more engagement with the content you are producing. With the majority of marketing being digital today, it's important to stand out and create something your customers will remember. Uberflip, for example, takes the idea of an online resource center and creates a continuous content experience that leads customer to read and discover related material.

Data enrichment and database health: Great marketing is predicated on having great data. Many companies make the mistake of investing in technology to help bring in leads but never think about how to make sure that data is accurate and actionable. Data enrichment providers help ensure that your data is up-to-date and can fill in the missing holes. For example, lead records in your system may be missing data such as company name, industry, revenue, and other important points. Data enrichment providers can take a single data point such as an email address and populate those missing fields. This enables you to level-up your segmentation and personalization efforts. Another great data tool choice is database health. Tools that perform deduplication and other data cleaning functions can turn an average database into a top performing one.

Creative assets builder: One category of Martech that you might not expect to be on this list is creative asset builder. These are tools that help you easily create emails, landing pages, and advertising campaigns using templates rather than have you code them from scratch. Digital marketing these days primarily takes place on digital assets such as these, and marketing teams often produce hundreds of assets over the course of the year. Rather than waiting on technical resources to create and customize, creative asset builders allow marketing teams to move swiftly and pivot when necessary. Tools like Unbounce not only allow you to create landing pages on the fly, but also run optimization experiments to improve conversion rates.

Summary

- Determine your marketing goals first and choose technologies that will help you achieve those goals.
- Focus on improving the customer experience and using Martech to make the experience better at each customer touchpoint.
- Identify Martech use cases by identifying business problems, surveying stakeholders, and speaking to agencies and peers.
- Select Martech vendors based on budget, critical needs, additional features, usability, and preference.
- One of the best ways to decide upon a Martech vendor is to run a successful pilot program.
- Great additional Martech to add is a webinar platform, content experience tool, data enrichment platform, and creative asset builder.

08

Principles for Robust and Scalable Martech Stack Management

In this chapter, we are going to cover the principles of robust and scalable Martech management. Many marketers mistakenly think that simply buying Martech will solve their problems, or that Martech will magically manage itself. This couldn't be further from the truth. While marketing technology has come a long way, it still takes considerable time and effort to effectively facilitate Martech in a way that drives profitable business results. All too often, marketers think that the act of buying a marketing automation platform will start yielding results in the next couple of weeks. In reality, the setup, configuration, integration and implementation of a marketing automation platform can take several weeks to months—and this is before the customer engagement activities start. Not to mention, there is a fair amount of technical expertise and cross-functional information you need to gather in order to properly set up a Martech platform.

Overarching Principles of Martech Management

There are high-level principles to think about before jumping into managing a Martech stack.

Goals: Remember that the purpose of a Martech stack is to help marketers achieve their business objectives. It is bad practice to add

Martech without a clear intention of how it will improve the customer experience, marketing efficiency, or actionable reporting. When setting up and managing your Martech stack, keep these questions in mind:

How can I create a stack that will…

- support the business goals of customer experience, revenue, efficiency, and reporting?
- empower and enable marketers to better engage our customers?
- enable data to flow and be available in all marketing platforms?
- protect and respect customer data and customer consent?

By reviewing your Martech goals and keeping those questions in mind, you will have laid the foundation of your team's successful use of marketing technology.

Robust and scalable Martech management: A common mistake is for marketers to set up their Martech stack in a way that serves a singular purpose in its present state, and doesn't prepare for multiple scenarios in the future. Marketing campaigns and marketing data never stay the same. You will always be adding more activities, more advertisements, more landing pages, more assets, and more data, so the tools in your stack should be configured to support a dynamic marketing environment and an ever-growing database. Keep these questions in mind when working with your Martech stack:

How can I create a tech stack that will…

- support our marketing for the next 3–5 years?
- support a marketing database several times the current size?
- support a large number of digital assets over time?
- support all the users in our marketing team in the future?

Think through these questions and others that you and your team come up with to build a robust and scalable Martech stack.

Technical Debt

Technical debt has been described as "what results when development teams take actions to expedite the delivery of a piece of functionality or a project which later needs to be refactored." (Productplan.com) For marketers, this refers to the amount of tedious and/or manual work that is created when they build marketing solutions or processes without thinking of long-term consequences. A great example is procrastinating on the integration of a webinar/event platform with the rest of your Martech stack. Without integration, all the attendees from each event must be downloaded from the webinar platform, cleaned and formatted, and then imported into each Martech tool that will utilize said data. Not only is this time-consuming, but it also creates more possibilities for error. Imagine a company that runs hundreds of virtual events per year—this creates a significant amount of extra work for the marketing team, and exposes the team to much unnecessary risk.

While the problem with technical debt is clear, it doesn't seem very obvious during implementation. Marketers typically want to move fast and get things done, so they may take the shortcut when it comes to using technology. The start of technical debt usually sounds like this: "Let's just do it this way this one time." But often, because of the desire to move quickly, the process is never revisited, and is repeated again and again over time. Another common example happens in reporting. Let's say that you need to match opportunities in your CRM with campaigns in your marketing automation platform. In the beginning, you may only have 20 opportunities in a given month, so downloading them from the CRM and cross-referencing them with campaigns in your MAP doesn't require much time. But the need for data and reporting is always constant, and will only increase. Before long, you are downloading hundreds of opportunities each month, and struggling to match them with campaigns in your MAP, taking up valuable bandwidth that you could use somewhere else. The manual activity that you are required to do each month is the technical debt, which could have been prevented by creating a solution or reporting mechanism that could match up the data automatically.

You can usually prevent technical debt from occurring by addressing two questions:

1 Is there a way we can elegantly automate this process?

2 Will this process be able to support our needs if the requirements were to grow several times?

While it is reasonable to have some technical debt, you can save yourself and your team unnecessary heartache by doing things right in the first place.

Who Should Own Martech?

It's important to clearly outline who owns marketing technology at your organization. This is critical for a number of reasons. First, having a single owner (or team that owns Martech) creates accountability for Martech, what the goals of each tool are, and forces business justification for each tool. For example, if a particular platform is not being used or is failing to generate optimal business results, the Martech owner can decide to remove it from the tech stack. Conversely, if the tech stack is missing a core functionality, or can be improved by adding a new tool, the Martech owner can make a case for procuring an additional tool. Second, a Martech owner can review the entire tech stack holistically, and ensure that the different components integrate with each other and properly support business objectives. When switching platforms or considering new platforms, the Martech owner can compare with the existing tech stack, the pros and cons of adding the platform, ensure there are no redundancies, and check that the new tech will fit in well with the existing tools. In addition, the Martech owner should also consider Martech usage and ROI for each individual tool.

There are several potential owners of the Martech stack.

Marketing operations: Marketing operations—the team responsible for the tools, processes, and data for the marketing team—should ideally own the Martech stack. This is because marketing operations typically work inside the technology the most; are the technology subject matter experts; and have an in-depth understanding of how the data flows between systems. Platform operations (sometimes referred to as system administration) is the function within the marketing operations group that typically owns the individual platforms—the group as a whole determines which tools to get rid of and which to add on.

Designated marketer: For smaller marketing teams that do not have a marketing operations function, Martech should be owned by a specific individual, with a clear charter to manage Martech and outline how Martech should support overall marketing objectives. Though this person will have additional responsibilities, they can serve as the go-to person when there are requests to add new tools. This person should be digitally savvy, and should presently be working with the tools on a day-to-day basis.

Information technology (IT): At many large companies it is common for IT to own Martech. It is organized this way because IT is responsible for many other work systems, such as servers, operating systems, databases, and more. They already have a software and technology budget and have the skills to administrate and govern platforms. Though this is common, it isn't necessarily ideal, because IT can sometimes be disconnected from marketing and business objectives, and may favor other goals such as stability, lower cost, and risk mitigation. Though those are not necessarily poor goals, they can be limiting to marketers looking to move quickly and find creative new ways to engage and market to customers. If Martech is owned by IT at your organization, it is important to set up an official working relationship to gain alignment around marketing goals and support. This is often referred to as a "dotted line" reporting relationship, meaning that there is no manager–subordinate connection; however, the parties have official responsibilities and deliverables to each other. It's also important to establish a regular cadence where marketing reviews technology owned by IT and identifies areas of improvement and optimization.

Centralized Ownership versus Decentralized Ownership

An important concept to think about in Martech is whether marketing platforms are owned centralized or decentralized. Central Martech ownership refers to a single team or group owning all of the marketing technology in terms of contract, budget, and administration. Decentralized ownership means that different teams can own the contract, budget, and administration of different tools. Let's talk about each one in detail.

Centralized Ownership

In a centralized ownership model, all of the Martech is owned by a single group. This is usually marketing or IT, and the key point here is that all of the new and existing Martech contracts run through this single group. One of the key benefits of this model is governance and redundancy limitation. Since all the Martech has a single owner, it is easier to see what Martech exists, who is using it, and who gets access to it. It is also much easier to see if there are any tools in the tech stack that serve the same purpose, or are doing duplicate work. Note that centralized ownership is much easier to facilitate in smaller organizations, for example, if there is only a marketing team of five employees, there is no reason for Martech ownership to be decentralized.

Decentralized Ownership

In a decentralized ownership model, marketing technology is owned by multiple groups. This is especially common if there are multiple marketing teams. For example, if there are different marketing teams for each region, let's say North America, EMEA, and APAC, each region could have their own set of tools, and they could be different from each other. Different teams can also use each other's tools, or sometimes even have the same set of tools but with different contracts. This decentralized model often happens when large organizations are trying to move quickly, or when mergers and acquisitions occur, meaning that the marketing teams were historically separate, and obviously would have a different tech stack. The benefits of decentralization are that teams can customize their tools for their unique needs faster, rather than having to wait for a central ownership group to acquire those tools for them. In many cases, central Martech owners may decline requests for additional tools if they do not see the business need.

Hybrid Ownership

It's not rare to see a combination of the centralized and decentralized Martech ownership models. In a hybrid model, larger platforms such as CRM and MAP are owned by a single group, such as the marketing operations team, and other smaller platforms may be owned by individual teams. This is especially common in large organizations where teams are separated by function. For example, there may be a marketing website team that is responsible for all marketing activities on the website. This team may employ specific tools for their needs which may not be particularly valuable to other groups that are working on different functions. It would make sense in this scenario for the marketing website team to procure this tool on their own without having to bother a central team about it.

Recommendations

The model that you employ at your company will be highly situational. For smaller companies such as startups, there really isn't another option besides centralized. For umbrella companies with completely different business units, it doesn't really make sense to centralize since the marketing activities are usually very different. Now for everything in between, note that it is much easier to deploy and manage and overarching Martech strategy with a centralized model. It is quite the undertaking to make sure tools integrate together, and that data flows between systems in a seamless way, and that tools provide unified reporting. It is much more difficult to manage a Martech strategy if disparate teams are purchasing tools without your knowledge and have mixed uses of the different tools in their stack.

SalesTech and Adjacent Tools

There are a growing number of tools adjacent to marketing technology, such as SalesTech, customer success tools, data tools, and more. While it is unlikely that there will be a marketing owner for these tools, it is important that you regularly review how your company uses different tools, if there is overlap, and how they work together. For example, it is possible for a customer to engage with assets that have been deployed through Martech and SalesTech, and both of those categories should be considered during attribution. Make sure to set up quarterly meetings with the owners of these adjacent tools to ensure a holistic and optimal customer engagement strategy and experience.

Managing Martech like Product Management

One effective way of managing marketing technology is to relate it to product management. In product management, product managers talk to users, prioritize features that they will use, and closely monitor products to optimize and make future improvements. In the same way, Martech managers can think about what Martech will create the best experience for their customers (both internally and externally), how to prioritize Martech platforms and projects, and how to optimize the tech stack in the future.

Starting with customers: Just as a product manager needs to understand the needs and motivations of their customer to create products and services that they will use and derive value from, Martech managers need to think about what external customers need from marketing and what internal stakeholders need to do their jobs better. For example, are customers getting the resources they need about your company's service? Can they easily navigate your site to find content, such as articles, tutorials, reports, and videos to serve their needs? If not, perhaps a resource management tool or content experience tool can help them in this area. What about your internal stakeholders?

Are they able to generate creative assets such as landing pages and emails quickly and with ease? If not, a self-service asset builder might be a way to drive efficiency in their process. The key thing to remember is that Martech should help both your internal and external customers achieve their goals.

Objectives and prioritization: Another thing product managers do is focus their work on creating features that will do the most good for internal and external customers. To do that, they look at all of the different objectives and features that they need to work on and prioritize them based on frameworks. You can apply these same principles when looking at different Martech tools and projects to work on. The RICE framework (reach, impact, confidence, effort) is an effective way to prioritize both tools and projects. Reach is how many users or customers that a tool will help. Impact is relative to goals and objectives, referring to how much it will help you achieve business goals. Confidence looks to minimize subjective opinion, referring to how much data you have that confirms the score of the other components of the framework. Effort refers to how difficult it will be to implement the tool or solution. By using the RICE framework formula, you can prioritize tools and projects that will help your team the most.

Feedback and iteration: Another thing Martech managers can borrow from product management is feedback and iteration. To seek feedback—both from stakeholders and from a results perspective—is to ask and investigate whether something is working or not. In marketing technology, this means to review the results of specific platforms by asking: Is this performing how we would expect? It also means talking to the users of platforms and asking: Is this platform serving the purposes you need and in an efficient way? Once you have feedback, this allows you to iterate based on that feedback. Iteration can come in the form of making slight modifications to platform configurations or integrations, or it can come in the form of migrating out entire platforms or groups of platforms. The spirit behind iteration is making changes to consistently improve and make progress.

Scope and workflow: After objectives and prioritization is complete, product managers work with technical resources to get the product produced. Many of these themes can translate over to marketing technology, because the implementation of tech requires scoping (understanding requirements and making plans to fulfil those requirements) and workflow, which speaks to managing the projects and work involved in building an effective tech stack. A typical example is the implementation of a new Martech platform. You'll start by scoping out the project; asking which data needs to be brought into the new system; which other tools the new platform needs to integrate with; and which people resources you will need to get this project done. As the system implementation launches, you set milestones and create regular check-ins to make sure your project is on track.

WHAT ARE THE SKILLS NEEDED TO MANAGE MARTECH?

We've been mentioning the needs for technical resources and people to manage Martech, and this is a good point to clarify what that means. Let's break these skills down into hard skills and soft skills.

Hard skills: Hard skills refers to technical skills in the same way that how hard data refers to exact numbers. There is a few key technical skills Martech managers need: competence in the basics of digital marketing, basic front-end web development, relational databases, and statistics. "Digital marketing basics" may sound broad, but refers to understanding how potential customers learn about your company through online channels, and how you nurture, convert, and delight customers through tactics like email, social media, mobile, and more. And while you don't need to become a programmer, it is very important to grasp the basics of front-end web development—specifically HTML, CSS, and JavaScript. You may not need to write coding scripts from scratch, but you should be able to read these languages and get a general idea of what the block of code does. Relational databases refers to databases with objects/tables that connect to each other. Almost all the tools in a Martech stack will use relational databases, and it is important to grasp the basics. Lastly, it's important to be versed in statistics—you should understand averages, standard deviations, probability, and statistical significance if you are to work in a data-driven profession like Martech.

Soft skills: The soft skills you need to manage Martech are cross-functional project management and clear communication. Most of the work you will do in Martech requires the help of multiple stakeholders, especially sales operations; sales and marketing; customer success; and technical resources such as product teams and engineers. Knowing how to influence these groups without authority is a critical skill you will need to get your work done.

Clear communication helps in any profession but is especially powerful in Martech. Being able to articulate clearly (especially in writing) the various benefits of marketing technology, and the things you need to integrate an effective tech stack will pay dividends long into the future.

Integrating Your Tech Stack

A very important concept is how your marketing technology stack integrates together. This refers to how data flows between separate systems, and the movement of data holistically to support the customer experience and business objectives. Martech integration is important because much of the value in Martech is predicated on having the right data, as well as said data being actionable in real time. For example, you can't send timely campaigns based on customer actions if one system doesn't know that the actions took place in another system. In addition, you can't make informed marketing decisions if the data in one platform isn't present in the centralized reporting tool. Making sure the data gets from one place to another is paramount to Martech success.

How Do You Successfully Integrate a Tech Stack?

You first must start by mapping your Martech stack and visualizing how the data should flow between the various components. By mapping, I mean documenting your tech stack in a visual format. A popular way to do this is with logos on a board or canvas. Each logo will represent a different tool in the Martech stack, and lines will be connected between each logo, which represents an integration/connection between two or more tools. The first map you want to think about is a customer journey map. This means you want to see data that you get from a customer based on their activities. For example, if a customer fills out a form on your website, which tool captures the data? Where does that data go? Where does that data sync to? Where does this data ultimately get reported on? In many cases, a form filled out on a website will take place in the CMS, get synched to the MAP and therefore the CRM, and ultimately be reported on in a data visualization tool such as Tableau or Domo. Now that you know how to connect tools together visually on a map, you can decide if this is the best way to connect the tools, which additional tools need to be brought into the mix, and if there are any efficiencies that can be gained by rearranging tools in the stack.

The next way that you can think about Martech integration is the facilitation of business reports. For example, every business needs a few key metrics to support business making, such as revenue, leads, meetings, opportunities, pipeline, and database size. All of these data points should feed into a centralized reporting tool. To plan this, create a new map, and this time place all your Martech logos and connect them in a way that shows how the data is moving toward the central reporting. Sometimes, tools must be connected first in order to get higher forms of data, such as marketing generated opportunities, which you can figure out by connecting the MAP and CRM together. It's worth mentioning that it is becoming increasingly popular to implement a centralized data tool, such as a customer data platform (CDP) to simplify this process. With the use of a CDP, all of the data from all tools that touch the customer are routed into a central database, and from that database update normalizations are made and sent back to each specific tool. In this version of the Martech map, the CDP is in the center, with all the other tools in the stack surrounding it in a circle.

Adding on Additional Tech to Your Stack

A big part of integrating a Martech stack is deciding on what is important when adding another system. The first thing to think about is native integrations. A native integration is a connection built by one or more of the tool providers, usually because integrating the tools in question together is very common. Native integrations tend to be more robust than custom integrations, and if there are any issues, you can rely on the support of the vendor to fix them. A native integration is ideal, but if that is not available, you should consider the level of effort required for a custom integration. A custom integration means that you are using two or more application programming interfaces (APIs) to get two systems to talk to each other. You can either build an integration yourself, hire a technical resource with an API, or you can use tools like Zapier, Tray.io, and Workato which give you a platform that allows you to manage API connections without having to code. Regardless of how you build an integration, keep in mind that some use cases require robust integrations. The integration between a MAP and a CRM, for example, should have a near real-time bidirectional sync to support timely customer engagement. Since it is quite difficult to build this type of integration yourself, a native integration would be the best option.

Tech Stack Automation

Finally, it's important to think about automating certain aspects of your Martech stack. While you should never automate everything in marketing, automating manual and repetitive tasks can be a big time-saver for your business. Automation can also help accelerate business-critical deliverables, such as speed-to-lead or speed-to-opportunity. A great example of tech stack automation is using a platform like Workato to trigger events in one platform based on an activity in another platform. For example, if a prospect fills out a contact-us form, Workato can create a task in the CRM, trigger an email in a MAP, and alert a sales rep in a chat platform such as Slack. Another great example is using a platform like Syncari to automate data normalization and synchronization. Data should be the same in different systems to support marketing in the best way. Syncari can take data in one system, format it in a way that is most usable for the business, and then make sure all corresponding systems have that same data in the same format. While there are many benefits to tech stack automation, make sure to monitor these automations carefully, and never take a "set it and forget it" mindset with automation.

Governance: User and Access Management

User and access management is an important concept in marketing technology, referring to which users have access to which systems and what level of access each user has. For example, salespeople may have access to the CRM, but not to any other marketing platform. Smaller use-case users may have read-only access to a MAP, but not have the ability to execute campaigns. Inexperienced users may have the ability to create assets in a content platform, but not to publish them. This concept is important because it limits risks. It also protects data and assets from a security perspective. A typical example of limiting risks is access to templates within a marketing platform. If an inexperienced user changes a template incorrectly, that could impact all future assets it is used to create. However, if that user does not have access to edit the template in the first place, the scope of their mistakes will be limited to their own assets. Another example, though hopefully rare, is the scenario of a "bad actor" with malicious intent. This could be an external third-party such as a malicious hacker or competitor, or a disgruntled employee. Without access management and platform security, this party could wreak havoc on systems and steal customer data.

How Do You Exercise Good User and Access Management?

The first thing you should think about is which users have access to which platforms. Users should only receive access to platforms that they need to perform their job. If a marketer, for example, does not need to publish blogs or view website analytics, they may not need access to a CMS. Next is the concept of a role, which is a set of access and permissions that a user has within a system. For example, the role of an administrator has access and permissions to do most tasks within a system, while the role of a standard user will be to only create and report on marketing campaigns. Administrators also have the ability to add and manage other users, which is another form of governance. Another common access-level is "read-only," which means that a user can view assets and data within a system—not edit them. The key concept here is read-access and write-access. Write-access means a user can edit (and usually delete) assets. Read-access is the ability to view assets, but not make any changes. Read-access is typically given to users that only need to see the data to generate reports or use the data for other initiatives. Beyond this, you can create many custom roles that have a mix of both read- and write-access, depending on your situation.

What Are Permission Sets and How Do They Differ from Roles?

Roles are really groups of permissions (capabilities) that users can perform, whereas permission sets can allow individual users to be given more capabilities or access without having to create a new role. Let's say you have three user roles: admins, standard users, and read-only users. In your role setup, only admins have write-access to templates. But one of your standard users has a great background in design and would greatly benefit the team if they can modify the templates. Rather than give that user admin access, or create a completely new role for the user, you can give them additional permission sets that allow this specific individual to have write-access to templates. This allows you to keep the overall role structure the same, but still benefit from users' unique capabilities.

SINGLE-SIGN-ON (SSO)
In talking about user governance and access management, it is important to bring up the concept of single-sign-on. Single-sign-on (or SSO) is an authentication method that enables users to securely authenticate with multiple applications and websites with just one set of credentials. In other words, users can log on one time, and have access to most if not all of the platforms in your Martech stack. This adds an additional layer of security, while also increas-

ing efficiency as users do not have to remember different sets of usernames and passwords. In addition, since users have one login set, they can automatically be blocked from all tools if they decide to leave the company. As your Martech stack grows and the volume of users increases, consider using SSO to simplify and elevate your user management.

Documenting Your Tech Stack

We've briefly covered documenting a flow-type diagram of your Martech stack earlier in this chapter, but since this is a very important concept we'll expand on it here. We'll cover three different examples and talk about the differing value each can bring to the organization.

Figure 8.1 shows a simplified example with a CDP in the middle. Notice how all Martech platforms in the stack connect to the CDP as the central platform. Martech stacks without a CDP may not have this hub-and-spoke structure and will likely have platforms that integrate with each other but not to all platforms in the stack.

FIGURE 8.1 Tech Stack Example

Wikis and Runbooks

While a Martech map is a great starting point toward Martech documentation, it is incomplete without written descriptions and instructions of how to operate the various components. Internal wikis and resource centers are great places to publish which marketing tools are being used; who owns each platform; and how to get support. Some companies go as far as having entire video libraries dedicated to training and support to help their users get up to speed on using different platforms. Runbooks are also great resources, and refer to step-by-step instructions with screenshots and references of how to operate specific tools and platforms, and are invaluable for changing organizations. Take for example, the case of employee turnover. What if a key Martech employee leaves, taking valuable knowledge of how to operate the Martech stack with them? This example underscores the need to have a well-documented Martech stack.

How to Create an Exceptional Martech Wiki

One of the best time investments you can make is to create a comprehensive Martech wiki. A wiki is a collaborative website or platform that multiple people can add content to—in this case you and your marketing team, and anyone else that can contribute useful information on marketing technology. This could include product managers, engineers, analysts, and many others. This is an important creation because a wiki serves as an internal resource for stakeholders, and is the go-to destination when users need to learn or need assistance with Martech. The wiki also hosts Martech platform documentation about who owns each platform and how each platform works, which is important information for the Martech team and anyone working on Martech projects.

There are many benefits to having a robust, central Martech wiki. First, the wiki is a self-service resource for users that can reduce burden on your platform administrators. As your organization grows, you will undoubtedly get many questions as to which Martech tools are available, how they are accessed, and how they are used. Without a Martech wiki, each of these questions would have to be fielded by your team, and you would have to respond with the same answers over and over again. A well-organized and updated wiki allows users to browse and search out these answers for themselves, and will have them returning repeatedly to serve as their field guide while they use the various marketing platforms. The additional benefit of a self-service wiki is that new employees can ramp up quickly, without needing to spend take too much time being trained by existing members. While new employees should always meet with existing team members for relationship building, there is often too much time wasted in conveying the same Martech information over and over again.

Martech wikis are exceptional training resources. While there are some Martech tools that are fairly intuitive, most need some training to get full adoption. Wikis allow users to learn at their own pace, and good wikis offer multiple mediums of training resources for deeper learning. Many marketers miss the fact that training other users helps multiply their efforts. If one marketer can use a suite of marketing tools to engage customers and drive business results, training others to repeat the process can compound those results. Wikis also can help users troubleshoot their own platform issues, which can save a lot of time for your team. Many platform problems can be caused by simple user error, and "frequently asked questions" can help users diagnose and resolve their own problems.

Instructions for Martech Wiki Creation

The first thing you need to create a wiki is a platform for hosting and editing. While you could use a website content management system (CMS) to host a wiki, it can be difficult to manage and train others to edit. Ideally, you'll want to pick a service that gives you the wiki management capabilities that allow you and multiple users to continually add and update content. Platforms like Confluence allow you to create multiple pages and sections to keep your information organized, while enabling users to edit content and leave comments to ask questions or to flag inaccurate information. If a paid platform isn't the best fit for your team, you can also use a shared file system such as Sharepoint or Dropbox to get much of the functionality you need.

Second, you want to list out the sections of the wiki that will work best for your organization. For smaller teams, a couple of pages with reference links will do, while enterprise companies will often have dozens of pages in their wiki. Another important point is that your wiki documentation should contain resources in as many different resources as possible. Martech training resources, for example, should be in written format, visual format, video, and live classes to account for the different ways that users learn and internalize new information.

Recommended Components

Here are some recommendations for key components of a Martech wiki. Keep in mind that this will greatly vary depending on your Martech stack and the number of stakeholders you are working with.

High-level team information: This component contains information about the Martech team and what its charter is. Keep this updated with information about each team member and their role in their team, how to get in touch with various members, and what scenario calls for outreach. You may want to include an ownership matrix on this page, which indicates who owns each marketing tool. This page is important so that stakeholders aren't lost trying to find a contact to get help with Martech, and also should set some boundaries as to what is in the Martech team's scope of responsibilities and what is not.

Roadmap: The roadmap component of the wiki provides all of the upcoming projects and work that the Martech team is looking to deliver in the nex year. This can be in the form of a simple list of projects with due dates and status updates, or it can be in visual format such as a Gantt chart. The roadmap is important for a couple of reasons. First, the roadmap lets stakeholders know what to expect from the Martech team in the months to come and can help them prepare resources or timelines to take advantage of products and features. Next, the roadmap gives an opportunity to highlight the Martech team's contribution to the business and showcase deliverables. Finally, it's also a method of time protection, as Martech teams can reference the roadmap when communicating how they are prioritizing work, and will help them say no to requests that are of lower priority.

Key reports: You should have a section of the wiki dedicated to the key marketing reports that the marketing platforms provide. This can include revenue reporting, marketing performance reporting, and also Martech systems reporting. This is important because it allows stakeholders to quickly access business critical reports, and also promotes transparency through the organization. Make sure to include instructions for how to access specific reporting platforms if necessary.

List of platforms and owners: Aside from the team information component, you can include a full page with a complete list of platforms and the corresponding owners. This is especially important if you have many Martech users in your organization who use multiple platforms. When they have platform-specific issues, they can reach out to the correct platform owner. This is also helpful if you have a large Martech stack, because users may not be aware of all the tools available to them.

Access requests: Another section to consider is an access request section, which includes rules and instructions to gain access to each platform. For some organizations, it is important to not let everyone have access to certain tools, to either protect customer data or for budgetary reasons. This section can also provide a description of the type of access users will get to each platform depending on their role, and how exactly they can request access. For example, it is common to set up a request intake system or process to request access.

Data dictionary: A Martech wiki should include a data dictionary, which is a glossary of terms and field descriptions that users of Martech should know. Terms can include platform-specific terminology, company jargon, and the names and descriptions of common fields like industry, job role, job function, usage, and many others. This is important because different platforms can use different terms and fields can be used for different purposes. A data dictionary helps

Martech stakeholders use a common lexicon when talking about Martech, and promotes better communication.

Training hub: The training hub is the section of the wiki that houses all of the assets and resources that help users learn the different aspects of Martech. This should include documentation on how to use each platform, as well as external resources such as vendor-created training. When bandwidth allows, you should have multiple versions/ mediums of training material. For example, when you produce an instructional guide on how to create a new email in a marketing automation platform, you should have a written version with screenshots, a video demonstration, links to vendor-documentation, as well as a schedule of live workshops that users can attend to learn. Having a training hub on your wiki is a great way to have an always on-demand channel for stakeholders to level-up their Martech skills.

Support tickets: The support tickets section of the wiki will describe when and how to submit requests to the Martech team for help. This should include the criteria of requests that can be submitted, such as who can submit requests and for which platforms and scenarios. It's also recommended to have service level agreements (SLAs) for support tickets, so users can know when their issue will be addressed. Without SLAs, users may become frustrated if they do not receive an immediate response, and it gives them a reason to follow up or escalate if the SLAs are not acceptable. If possible, try to set up your support intake system in a way that automatically assigns requests to the correct team member, which can be done by customizing the fields and workflow of support requests in the associated support platform.

Office hours: Martech teams that support large organizations should hold regular office hours, which are regularly scheduled sessions where users can show up and get help on Martech issues. For example, users can attend office hours to help troubleshoot a campaign they are trying to deploy through Martech, or to learn how to use a tool for the first time. The section of the wiki dedicated to office hours will explain to users when and how to sign up for office hours, and will provide a schedule for the upcoming time period.

Marketing compliance and consent: A component of the wiki should be dedicated to marketing compliance and consent, which explains how customer data is captured, processed, and used in marketing activities, as well as how customer consent is operationalized in the various Martech platforms. This section of the wiki is important because of the legality of the topics, as well as to inform users of the latest data and compliance policies.

Data Security and Compliance

This is an important section of this chapter, but it is important to note that the advice given in this book should not be considered legal advice, and it is recommended that you become informed on these topics by reviewing the official rules and regulations for marketing and data compliance in your jurisdiction, as well as speak to an attorney if appropriate.

What is data security, compliance, and consent? Data security refers to protecting user and customer data within your systems from any type of bad actors or parties with malicious intent. Compliance refers to adhering to the rules and regulations of the governing entities that legislate laws and guidelines for each country, and consent refers to gaining permission from consumers about how their data is used.

Why are these topics important? At a high level, these topics deserve special consideration since going against these rules and regulations can result in fines and at worst can be considered criminal acts. Organizations all over the world have been forced to pay fines of hundreds of millions of dollars for not following the guidelines that we'll be outlining. At a deeper level, respecting and protecting consumer data should be a moral standard and is essential to maintaining trust with our customers. From a tactical level, not following guidelines such as GDPR and CAN-SPAM results in sender reputation and deliverability issues, as well as increases in unsubscribes, which impacts your mailable database.

How can you keep your data secure? The first thing to review is your own internal practices. Do your databases have the proper firewalls and security mechanisms in place? Do you have user permissions and access management policies that limit risk and protect your data from bad actors? These basic security protocols can go very far in terms of keeping your data secure. The next thing you want to review is the vendors where you store your data or have access to your data. This includes marketing technology vendors and agencies or contractors that work with your team. These vendors should have clear documentation around how the keep their own data secure, because if they suffer a data breach, it is your data that gets exposed. Second, you should make sure you have a data processing agreement (DPA) in place, which is a legal contract that states how the data in question will be stored and used, and if the practices abide by regulations such as GDPR.

How do you stay compliant? There are various rules and regulations that you need to know. We have listed some here, but we recommend you speak to an attorney before you conduct your marketing to make sure you understand these topics and how they specifically apply to your organization and industry.

GDPR: Though the General Data Protection Regulation (GDPR) was drafted and passed by the European Union (EU), it imposes obligations onto organizations anywhere, so long as they target or collect data related to people in the EU. The regulation was put into effect on May 25, 2018. The GDPR will levy harsh fines against those who violate its privacy and security standards, with penalties reaching into the tens of millions of euros. Some of the notable rules in the GDPR are the requirement of expressed consent, and the right to be forgotten. (Since "Brexit", GDPR has been carried over into UK law.)

CAN-SPAM: US Congress enacted the Controlling the Assault of Non-Solicited Pornography and Marketing ("CAN-SPAM") Act in 2003 to set a national standard for the regulation of spam email. Among other things, the CAN-SPAM Act of 2003 prohibits the inclusion of deceptive or misleading information and subject headings, requires identifying information such as a return address in email messages, and prohibits sending emails to a recipient after an explicit response that the recipient does not want to continue receiving them. CAN-SPAM makes it illegal to send unsolicited marketing messages.

CASL: A new Canadian anti-spam law, CASL, will apply to all electronic messages (i.e. email, texts) organizations send in connection with a "commercial activity." Its key feature requires Canadian and global organizations that send commercial electronic messages (CEMs) within, from, or to Canada to receive consent from recipients before sending messages. CASL does not apply to CEMs that are simply routed through Canada.

CCPA: The California Consumer Privacy Act (CCPA) is legislation designed to improve the data privacy of California residents. It gives citizens the right to know when and how their information is being collected and sold, as well as the ability to opt out. It also grants them legal right to the same service and price of service whether or not they exercise their privacy rights.

What is Marketing Consent?

Marketing consent refers to how companies can store, track, and use consumer data. The best examples of this are email and digital cookie tracking. Consumers need to opt-in to be emailed, and they need to give consent for them to be tracked online via cookie. To keep this easy to understand, we are going to talk about the different types of marketing consent as it applies to email marketing.

Expressed consent: Expressed consent is when the consumer has actively given you permission to send them marketing emails. This is typically done with a checkbox that the consumer has to click on to check, which signals opting into marketing communication.

Implied consent: Implied consent means that there is a business relationship between the company and the consumer, therefore a company can send the consumer marketing emails without "expressed consent" given by the consumer. The typical example of this is that companies are allowed to send marketing emails to their existing customers.

Compulsory consent: Compulsory consent, which is the type of marketing consent used in Japan, means that companies cannot collect the email address of the consumer without the consumer agreeing to receiving marketing messages. A typical example of this is presenting a form to a consumer, and not allowing the consumer to submit their information unless they agree to receiving marketing communication.

Double opt-in: There are some countries, such as Germany, that require consumers to double opt-in to receive marketing emails. This means that upon submitting their information, consumers will receive a confirmation email that they have to actively click to confirm they want to receive marketing emails from the organization.

Make sure to consult legal resources in your jurisdiction before conducting your marketing to make sure you are marketing in a compliant way.

How Do You Operationalize Marketing Consent?

There are two key parts to making sure your organization abides by the marketing consent of consumers: building an effective preference center and creating data programs and processes that align with marketing consent.

Preference center: A preference center is an online landing page/form that allows consumers to tell organizations the types of emails they would like to receive from them. It allows them to subscribe to specific communication types such as newsletters, offers, invitations, and more, and also allows them to unsubscribe from all marketing communications completely. Some preference centers offer other customizations, such as allowing consumers to select the timing and frequency of marketing messages, as well as enabling them to opt in to receiving messages from approved partners. Regardless of how many preferences you let your consumers choose from, having a robust and functional preference center is paramount to respecting consumers' marketing consent.

Managing marketing consent data: Once you have the data that tells you which types of communication your consumers have opted in to, it's important to operationalize that consent by building programs to make sure consumers only receive the messages they have subscribed to. While there are many ways to do this depending on the marketing platform you are using, the key is to suppress/exclude consumers from messages based on their consent. For example, your setup should prevent marketers from sending messages to consumers that have unsubscribed, and depending on the campaign type, exclude consumers that have not opted into the content of said campaign.

Summary

- Goals for a Martech stack are customer experience, revenue, and scalable and robust Martech management.
- Martech should have a clear owner, and it is important to consider whether you should centralize or decentralize Martech ownership.
- Make sure to facilitate owning Martech like a product manager, keeping in mind your goals and users as you build out your tech stack.
- Making sure your tech stack integrates together is paramount for effective Martech management.
- Invest in documenting your Martech stack, with map diagrams, wikis, and runbooks.
- Data security and marketing compliance cannot be overlooked. Prioritize making sure you protect your customers data, and adhere to their preferences.

09

Martech Measurement, Governance, and Enablement

Martech Measurement

The importance of measurement goes back to the Peter Drucker quote in his seminal book *On Management*, "What gets measured, gets managed" (Drucker, 1970). Many marketers make the mistake of putting Martech in place without having a way to report on its performance, and what can be improved. Martech measurement can be a confusing topic, because there are two dimensions in which we need to look at measurement and reporting. First, there is general marketing reporting, which refers to the business side of marketing reports. Next is the reporting on Martech systems themselves, including system performance, usage, troubleshooting, and efficiency. We'll cover both of these in this section.

Marketing Reporting

Revenue reporting: Marketing reporting refers to measuring how marketing is performing and the contribution it is making to the business. The best way to start thinking about marketing reporting is a top-down approach. Keep in mind that most of marketing applies to top-line revenue, which equates to sales. The first report you need is a revenue report, and this report shows where the sales come from in the business. Sales can come from new business (new customers), and renewals and upsells (customers). This can be further broken down into sources of sales, which are the sales team; partners; servicing and consulting for current customers; and marketing. Your business may have even more sources, but these are the most common. Even though you are mostly concerned with marketing, it is a good idea to track where all revenue comes from to gain a better understanding of how marketing contributes to that revenue. When it comes to revenue that comes from marketing, you want to track revenue that was sourced from marketing (marketing generated the lead that eventually purchased), and deals that were influenced by marketing (leads that came in from a different source, but converted because of engagement through a marketing program). Make sure to keep a clear definition of what "marketing-influenced" means at your organization, because it is often considered a softer metric that is easily changed to frame marketing in a better light. You don't want to appear as if you are changing reports to give your team more credit.

Marketing performance reporting: A step below revenue reporting is marketing performance reporting. This refers to measuring the effectiveness and efficiency of marketing channels and programs. First come your channel reports. How do each of the marketing channels contribute to revenue and brand awareness? These channels include your website, advertising, social media, email, direct mail, and more. You need to measure the results each channel generates such as opportunities, leads, subscribers, and engagements. By measuring the performance of channels, you can compare them against each other and identify ways to optimize each one. Next is your campaigns and programs. We'll define campaigns as a time-bound marketing initiative, such as an event or an offer, and we'll define programs as an evergreen marketing initiative such as a community or educational nurture series. Similar to channel reporting, you need to measure all of the results that come from each campaign. In addition, you can measure the ROI of each campaign since there is typically a spend associated with each one. Programs can be more challenging to measure, as they may not lead directly to revenue, but it is important to measure the growth of programs such as members-added and engagement levels, because it can make a significant impact on your brand awareness and customer sentiment. Marketing performance reporting is a more tactical form of reporting compared to revenue reporting, but is still very important to ensuring your marketing success.

MARKETING ATTRIBUTION

It's difficult to talk about marketing reporting without covering the topic of marketing attribution. Marketing attribution is assigning credit to various marketing initatives. For example, if a marketing campaign generated a sale of $1,000, you can attribute $1,000 of credit to said marketing campaign. Marketing attribution is a way for marketers to improve their investment decisions. Smart marketers will use marketing attribution to determine their top performing channels and campaigns and optimize their spend accordingly. The problem with marketing attribution is twofold: first, marketing attribution only applies to touchpoints that can be tracked. This is easier for social media, website traffic, and email marketing, but more difficult when it comes to word-of-mouth marketing, branding, and referrals. Second, marketers often make the mistake of using marketing attribution to demonstrate marketing's effectiveness. In other words, marketers will try to prove their worth to the business by using marketing attribution. This is not a good idea, because marketing attribution is not an exact science, and can be confusing to leadership and to finance. Marketers need to keep that in mind, and remember to use marketing attribution as one of the sources that help them make better decisions.

Cadence of marketing reporting: In a LinkedIn poll of 522 marketers, 43 percent said they review marketing reports weekly, while 29 percent said they review marketing reports daily (Figure 9.1).

Depending on the size of your organization, you will need to figure out how often to share reports with stakeholders and leadership. For smaller companies where most teams have a finger on the pulse of what is going on, a simple email with report highlights may suffice. For larger organizations where hundreds of people are unfamiliar

FIGURE 9.1 LinkedIn Poll Results

How often do you review marketing reports?

You can see how people vote. **Learn more**

Daily	29%
Weekly ✓	43%
Monthly	20%
Quarterly	7%

522 votes · Poll closed · **Remove vote**

with the results marketing is reporting, sharing reports becomes a much more formal undertaking. At minimum, you should prepare a quarterly business review (QBR) for marketing, which is a formal presentation and/or document that shares marketing goals, progress toward goals, contribution to the business, and major initiatives. To a smaller group, you definitely want to have monthly meetings which highlight how marketing is trending toward more tactical goals, such as traffic growth or lead growth. Now we will move onto covering Martech systems reporting.

Martech Systems Reporting

Martech systems reporting refers to measuring the effectiveness and efficiency of the platforms and tools in your Martech stack. This includes system performance, usage and limits, efficiency, and errors. Keep in mind that Martech systems reporting is more useful for larger platforms such as a MAP, CRM, CMS, and/or CDP, compared to point solutions that only perform a single or few functions.

System performance: When it comes to Martech, system performance refers to how a platform uses resources and how efficiently it performs its designated function. In many marketing platforms (especially at large organizations) system speed can significantly deteriorate due to poor administration. In a specific example, if you have a large marketing automation database and many workflows running simultaneously, customer campaigns and stakeholder experience can be impacted. You may have to request system performance reports from your Martech vendor; however, you can monitor system usage, as well as how many events/activities occur over a given time period. It's also a good idea to get first-hand experience of how efficiently a platform is running by regularly performing basic tasks. For example, by running sample reports and activating assets and campaigns, and seeing how long each task takes.

System usage and limits: It's a good idea to see how much of the system you are using, and how close to your account limits you are. For example, for your video marketing platform, how many videos are you hosting and how many reports are you running? How close are you to your account/plan's limits? For some platforms, a large amount of assets will not impact system performance, but for some platforms they do, and in those cases you want to deprecate assets that you are no longer using.

System efficiency: System efficiency refers to how fast your system executes certain tasks. For smaller tools and tasks, this isn't as important. System efficiency becomes very important for large tasks such as database reporting and running extract transform load (ETL) tasks. For example, if you are importing or exporting a database of millions of records, an efficient system will be able to do it in a much more reasonable time frame. You may have to request system efficiency metrics from your vendor, but regardless, it's a good idea to know that your system is running smoothly and that you have the ability to run large scale workflows or data changes if you need to.

Errors: Another thing that you should keep track of is the number of large scale errors that occur within each platform. While this will probably be negligible for smaller tools, robust platforms that support enterprise companies commonly have medium to large scale errors on a regular basis. Problems, issues, and errors are usually categorized from 1–5, with 1 being an error so large that the entire platform doesn't work, and 5 being a very minor issue that should be resolved before it causes a greater impact. Here are more detailed definitions:

- Problem Category 1: The entire marketing platform is not working in a large capacity, also known as "production down."

- Problem Category 2: The error is large enough that it is causing a negative impact to customers. For example, an issue is causing customers to see a blank content block on a landing page.

- Problem Category 3: An error is impairing the productivity of a group, for example, several users are not able to build a campaign.

- Problem Category 4: A single user is impaired from completing tasks on the platform.

- Problem Category 5: A minor issue that does not impair the productivity of users.

Especially for larger organizations, you should track the number of issues that occur with your Martech platforms each month, and what the severity levels are. If you find your team is experiencing several high-severity issues each month, it may be time to make some large process or platform changes.

Cadence of Martech systems reporting: Since Martech systems reporting has a more niche audience, you can stick to quarterly reports for sharing with your audience. Your quarterly reports should give an overview of the status of projects that happened during the quarter, and what the roadmap looks like for the next three quarters. Additionally, make sure to produce an abbreviated version of the quarterly reports for a monthly report that can be viewed by a more technical audience. Very often, a newsletter-style update will work for this monthly report.

Governance

Now we are going to deep-dive into Martech governance. We briefly talked about governance when we covered user permissions, but there is a lot more to it that can have significant ramifications on the long-term health and success of your tech stack. The key thing that we are going to be talking about when we think of governance is ensuring that users are accessing and utilizing Martech in a compliant, secure, scalable, and effective way.

There are a number of consequences that can occur if we are too lackadaisical about Martech governance. First, we open up our technology to the risk of bad actors. This could be internal or external parties that wish to harm our business or customers in some way. For example, without governance, a disgruntled employee could broadcast an inappropriate message on a company's social media networks. Next, poor governance can expose customer data. While employees may have the best of intentions, we do not want to share customer data with every employee unnecessarily. Customer data should be treated with privacy and respect. Let's say we have a customer's internet preferences and address in our system—only employees with the need to view that data should have access to it. Finally, governance prevents mistakes from getting out of hand. One of my teams referred to this as "limiting the blast radius." Let's say a marketing campaign was set up incorrectly, and instead of targeting a specific audience it targeted everyone. With effective governance, you can limit the total audience size of a given campaign to a specific region or to maximum audience size, so even if there was a mistake, it is much smaller than would have been without governance.

How to Limit the Blast Radius

Here is how you can limit the blast radius in your tech stack. Follow this rule: all users should only have the minimum amount of platform and data access to do their job. For small teams of three people or less, you don't really have to worry about this rule, there isn't much ROI there. However, as your team scales, this rule will become increasingly important. Here is a an example: from a platform perspective, if a marketer's role is to only send out email, they should only be given access to the tools required to their job. This may include the MAP, CRM, and DAM platform, but may not include platforms that manage social media, video marketing, website content, and more. From a data perspective, a marketer that only needs to see if conversions are up or down, doesn't need to see the individual names and contact information. Make sure that their access to the information enables them to see the high-level metrics of their campaign, but not access to personal identifiable information (PII).

Governance documentation: You should create a stakeholder-facing document that explains what each level of access/permissions users need to receive and why. Ideally, this will be a matrix outlining the type of platforms, permission levels, and data access each user needs depending on their role.

Governance buy-in: You'll need buy-in from leadership to be able to enforce the governance on users. In other words, without clear support from leaders that have influence over the entire organization, it will be likely your users will argue with you for additional access. Create a document or presentation that explains the concepts of these chapters so you can get clear approval from leadership to enforce Martech governance.

HOW TO HANDLE A HOSTILE TAKEOVER OF YOUR MARTECH STACK

All too often you will find yourself at odds with stakeholders who want to change the way Martech works at your organization. This could be buying additional tools without vetting them first, or using marketing platforms in ways that they are not supposed to be used. For example, it is very common for engineering or customer success stakeholders to want to send critical communications through an email marketing platform or marketing automation platform. Because these platforms often use a shared email server, where multiple businesses share the same server, this can create deliverability issues that are difficult to solve. But stakeholders will persist because email and marketing automation are some of the easiest ways to deliver messages to customers. For this and many other cases, you need strategies to deal with conflicting demands made of your Martech stack.

Focus on business goals: Often, stakeholders will request products or features to "try something new" or to increase efficiency. While those are not malicious requests, there is more to business and marketing success than experimentation and efficiency. What many stakeholders forget is that Martech teams are continually strapped for resources, and making one decision to buy a platform or support a feature often means foregoing another. This is why it is important to clearly state the goals you have for marketing and for your Martech stack, and have a clear roadmap of what you will be working on for the year. When a new tool or project comes up, you can easily compare it to your existing goals and roadmap, and make a decision if a trade-off should be made.

Check your resources: Not only do you have a finite budget, but you also have a finite team. Implementing new tools and features always takes talent and time, and if your team is busy always taking on new requests, they'll never have time to work on the most important initiatives for the business. Managing resources is an important skill: create a list of the different projects each of your team members is working on, and indicate how much bandwidth each person has for additional work. Only when you are sure you aren't sacrificing important deliverables for key projects should you take on additional requests for new platforms and features.

Apply long-term thinking: Most tool and feature requests are made to solve an immediate problem. When you give way to too many of these requests, you end up with a chaotic tech stack and several unused platforms. The key to solving this problem is to think long-term. Will the problem that we are facing continue to be a problem tomorrow? How about next year? If we implement a new tool, what kind of value can we expect to get out of it in the future? Are there additional benefits beyond solving a single problem? Questions like these can help frame your problems in a more accurate light, and can help you make the right decisions when it comes to implementing short-term solutions.

FIGURE 9.2 Escalation Communication

Escalate when appropriate: When all else fails, it helps to have executive buy-in. This is why it is important to get agreement on goals and roadmap at the beginning of the year; this way you can re-confirm what the priorities are, and make a case to protect your time. Here is a great way to make a case to executives (Figure 9.2).

1 **Situation**: Explain briefly what the issue is, and any context necessary to understand the situation.
Example: The partner marketing team wants to implement a new tool to track email signature clicks.

2 **Risk**: State the risk of taking on the project in terms of what the business will be losing out on.
Example: The new email signature tracking software will require an additional $500 per month and will require 20 hours of technical resources including changing our email server, integration with other platforms, and training of users. Allocating the 20 hours to this new project will push back the delivery date of our lead routing improvement project which should deliver leads to sellers in half the time (this example is a bit extreme, but the emphasis is to quantify the risk).

3 **Alternative**: Offer up multiple interim solutions and agree to revisit the topic when appropriate.
Example: To help the partner marketing team track activity on their email signatures, we can create a tracking link with our existing marketing platform, and deliver reports to them on a regular basis. In addition, we can revisit purchasing email signature tracking software next quarter during our technology review.

Bonus note: One tip that I use is to require stakeholders to write up a business justification document for any new features or platforms that they want implemented. Often this is a sufficient deterrent for stakeholders in making unnecessary requests, because writing the document requires substantial consideration of the challenges and necessity of the request in question.

Five Big Ideas When it Comes to Governance

Governance is a tricky thing. In reality, it means that you are setting out rules on how to use your technology stack, and enforcing those rules on stakeholders. This can be highly contentious, especially at organizations where users want to move quickly and are tasked with big goals. How do you employ governance in your organization without being a roadblock for everyone? Here are five ideas to help you.

Decide upon a north star: A "north star" consists of one or two sentences that describe the mission of your team. This can be very helpful because you can refer to it when you have to make tough decisions. An example of a north star statement could be: "The mission of our Martech team is to empower stakeholders to create delightful marketing experiences that drive business value for customers and our organization." This way, you can compare your goals and projects to your north star mission, and see if they align. This is also a great way to make sure your team and cross-functional teams understand what the purpose of your group is and what your long-term objectives are. When thinking about taking on new projects, using Martech for new use cases, or supporting different things, always ask: "Does this align with our north star?"

Use tenets for clarity: Tenets are written statements that your team agrees upon that address how you will handle contentious topics. Spend some time brainstorming what types of decisions you will have to make that may cause some controversy. Keep in mind your north star, and get buy-in from leadership on your tenets.

Here are some sample tenets:

- We strive for revenue goals, but hold customer experience in the highest regard.
- We implement connected and scalable technology with intention and purpose.

- We experiment regularly, but strive for robust reliability.
- We use technology that aligns with our long-term vision.
- We value people, process, and technology, in that order.

Draft your tenets and get input from each of your team members.

Win over power users: In order to make sure your rules and policies are adopted, you need to gain the confidence of power users. Power users are stakeholders that heavily use marketing technology, and are usually very vocal about their opinions and identifying problems that arise. One helpful strategy is to have a monthly meeting to gather feedback from power users about the tools they are using and what their pain points are. Take the opportunity in these meetings to cover new policies and the reasons behind them, that way they can explain and champion the governance initiatives out to the broader user base. Power users are also a great sounding board for new policies, they can give their opinion on policies ahead of time before you officially roll them out.

Training as a means of earning permission: An elegant way to manage governance, such as permissions and user access, is to use training as a means of earning permission. This refers to only allowing users to access certain platforms and certain features after they have gone through training. If you have sufficient resources to create training material, you can have users take internal live classes or on-demand training and even check their knowledge with scored examinations. If you don't have the bandwidth to produce training yourself, check with your Martech vendors as to what training resources they can provide. Some of the larger service providers, such as CRM and MAP providers, offer their own industry certifications. Requiring that a user become certified in a particular technology might be a little overboard, but consider using certification resources to teach your users to make sure they understand the tools before using them.

Solicit constant feedback: We briefly covered this in the section about power users, but will underscore it here. Many Martech managers forget that without people (users) there would be no point in having marketing technology. You always need to get buy-in and think about people, process, and technology together. Soliciting feedback from power users is a great start, but you need to be regularly asking for feedback from the entire user base. Create a quarterly all-user survey that goes out to everyone who uses Martech at your company to gauge the sentiment about Martech and what the pain points are. Here are some ideas for questions:

- Which tools/platforms do you use the most?
- Which tools/platforms do you need more training on?
- Do you find X tool easy to use?
- Do you find X tool effective for helping you get your work done?
- On a scale of 1–10, how would you rate the support you receive regarding X tool?
- On a scale of 1–10, how would you rate the training you took on X tool?
- What are your biggest pain points regarding our tech stack?

Use these questions as a baseline, and add more of your own. You'll be surprised at the insights you receive from this survey, and your work will benefit from being very aligned with your stakeholders.

Enablement

Enablement refers to helping users use marketing technology to achieve their goals. This includes training, support, and managing project requests. Many Martech managers make the mistake of equating enablement with documentation, but documentation is only a piece of the puzzle.

Running the Support Function

As your business scales, you will have to support dozens (sometimes hundreds) of users who depend on your Martech stack. As previously mentioned, documentation will not be enough to help users; you will have to interface with them directly. The first thing you want to do is create a support ticket system to manage bugs, system errors, or training requests. Ideally, you will want to use a workflow management platform such as Jira or Workfront to properly intake and assign these tickets. If you don't have a workflow management platform, consider using the ticket feature of a customer service tool or a case tool in a CRM to manage these requests. Your last resort would be to use a makeshift intake system, using a combination of Google forms or similar low-priced intake tool, and email communication. The key is to move support requests from personal channels such as email and instant message, because that is where they can easily get lost.

The next step is to create an ownership matrix or RACI chart. An ownership matrix outlines which team member is responsible for which system, and who is responsible for each individual part of the system. This way you can assign tickets to the assigned individual when they come in. A RACI chart lists out who is responsible, accountable, consulted, and informed about each platform. This may be a little excessive for a support function, but may be useful for larger projects versus minor requests.

Lastly, you want to establish a daily standup with your Martech team to go through the support tickets. A standup is a brief meeting (usually 10—20 minutes) with all team members where you quickly discuss issues, roadblocks, and collaboration opportunities. This specific standup meeting will address the incoming support tickets and who will own them. My recommendation is to have this standup meeting as early in the day as possible, that way you will get the highest attendance. In the standup meeting, have one team member share their screen and call out the tickets one by one. There may be times where you are tempted to try and solve one of the issues during the meeting, but try not to do this. Unless there is a high-severity issue, assign each ticket to a team member, and have the team member set up offline meetings to work out solutions. You will find that the practice of having a daily standup keeps your team very aligned, and also helps with unblocking your team by keeping communication strong.

How to Manage Escalations

There are two types of escalations you want to think about when supporting your stakeholders. One is escalations you make to the Martech vendor, and the other is escalations you make to your own hierarchical chain (your manager, skip-level manager, department VP etc.). In terms of escalating to Martech vendors, it is a good idea to allow your power users to access vendor support directly, otherwise you will become the intermediary in transferring messages back and forth. Next, let vendor support know as soon as possible when there are problems with your tech platforms. Though vendor support may give you a hard time about smaller issues, the reality of the situation is that it is their job to be aware of and investigate problems and to help their customers. You are paying them after all! Next you want to think about how to escalate issues in your own company. With many issues, the escalation path will lead to the owner of the Martech stack. This could be the Martech team leader, or perhaps the director/VP of digital marketing. However, when there are large scale outages, such as a key platform going down, don't be afraid to escalate to marketing leadership. Leadership should be informed when key parts of their business are at risk, and it will be helpful to have their support if you decide to switch vendors, or hire agencies to help you with issues.

Building and Managing a Center of Excellence

A key part of enablement is building and managing a center of excellence. A center of excellence is a collection of campaign templates, asset templates (such as email), process templates, experiment templates, and really anything that marketing uses that can be leveraged again and again by the marketing organization. The purpose of a center of excellence is first, to create efficiency by having ready-made templates for marketers to use, and second, share best practices across the organization by consistently improving the templates. So how do you build a center of excellence? The first step is to take a single campaign or program, and make sure that it is complete in all aspects. This is often referred to as an end-to-end process or workflow. Take an email campaign for example: you'll want to have a customer list, two versions of an email for an A/B test, a landing page with an offer, and a report. Take the most effective versions of each of these, and put it into your center of excellence where others can access and copy it. In a MAP, this is very easy, since the platform will allow you to copy or replicate campaign templates. For non-MAP components, you will need to store them in a DAM or file storage tool such as Dropbox or Sharepoint. Repeat this process for all the different initiatives that marketing has, and this will make up your center of excellence. One thing not to forget is process templates. Let's say you often intake requests for features or new projects. Make sure to have an intake template that you use repeatedly to ensure you are capturing necessary requirements and are not having to reinvent the wheel every time.

Next you need to enforce the use of the center of excellence. A center of excellence is only as good as how often it is used. Train your marketers and document the process so everyone knows that instead of building campaigns from scratch, they need to utilize a premade template in the center of excellence. For those that tend to skirt the rules, meet with them and ask what they are missing from the center of excellence. Take steps to fill in the gaps and your users will very much appreciate that. Lastly, you want to schedule time to review your center of excellence regularly. Monthly is ideal, but do it quarterly at a minimum. In each review, ask:

1 How is each template performing?

2 How do we know?

3 Which template can be improved?

4 How are users adjusting the templates to better suit their needs? Could those modifications become the norm?

5 What experiments have been run on the templates? What did we learn from those experiments that we can include as part of the stand templates?

By continually reviewing and improving your center of excellence, you will ensure the quality of your campaigns and programs improve over time, instead of declining over time.

Summary

- Measure both marketing performance reporting and marketing system performance reporting.
- Governance is an important part of effectively managing Martech, don't skip it.
- You can prevent a hostile takeover of your Martech stack by focusing on goals, resources, long-term thinking, and by escalating when appropriate.
- Be thoughtful about governance, write out a north star and tenets for your team.
- Running a support function effectively is critical to Martech enablement success.
- The key to ensuring your Martech programs get better over time is building and managing a center of excellence.

10

Getting Buy-In

This chapter is going to be all about getting buy-in for your marketing technology as well as your overall Martech strategy. Let's first define what "getting buy-in" really means. Getting buy-in means that you have the support and approval of the different key leaders, stakeholders, users, and other adjacent teams that will be using Martech. You have their support, cooperation, and overall understanding of why you're going to be implementing a particular Martech tool or strategy. This also means that you have agreement and financial support to secure resources, time, and anything else you may need to implement and execute a new Martech strategy. Having each of these components means you have succeeded in getting buy-in.

Let's look at a simple example. Say you need marketing leadership and finance to approve the budget to purchase a new marketing automation platform or to migrate to another marketing automation platform. At the stakeholder level, getting buy-in means that the different marketers in your organization are aware that you are going to purchase a new marketing automation platform. They are informed about the change, and are ready to do the work necessary to make the change happen. Keep in mind that stakeholders may not always agree with changes, at least initially, but it's important to ensure that the different parties you are working with aren't openly hostile against your initiative.

It's also important to get buy-in from adjacent teams. In the marketing automation platform example, you want to secure buy-in from not just marketing, but also sales and sales operations. These adjacent teams should be informed and aware, as well as understand the role that they're going to play in the rollout of this new Martech strategy.

Why is Getting Buy-In for Martech Important?

There are three key reasons why getting buy-in for Martech is important.

Resource needs: Martech projects require budget, both from a monetary and technical resource standpoint. For example, say you are going to be migrating to a new marketing automation platform. In order to successfully deliver this project, you are going to need the support of sales operations, as well as other technical integration resources, to transfer your database to another platform and complete the proper configurations. It's also common to need additional budget for outside help, which will need to get approved by marketing leadership and finance. Without this, your project will stall.

People needs: In terms of stakeholders, many people forget that marketing and business in general is all about people. It's going to be people that actually work with the different tools: setting them up, setting up campaigns, and setting up customer engagements. At the end of the day, ROI is driven with these tools, and if people do not buy-in—and if they're not supportive of the technology—the platforms and applications could go unused and become shelfware (sitting on the metaphorical shelf).

The final reason why getting buy-in is so important is that you want to get in tune with how the stakeholders feel about the marketing technology, what their sentiment is about using the marketing technology, and if it's effective and performing the way you/they want it to. If you don't, this is valuable feedback that is missed out on.

One story that illustrates the importance of these needs was my rollout of the LinkedIn Sales Navigator across a global sales organization. LinkedIn Sales Navigator is an online platform that helps salespeople prospect and build relationships across LinkedIn in a more effective way, allowing them to build lists of prospects, get information on key contacts and accounts, and send messages in the form of emails to prospects to try to create engagement and set up meetings.

I knew that we wouldn't get the budget to purchase this tool if we didn't get buy-in from the sales leadership and salespeople, so I set up a kickoff call with sales and several training sessions to teach them how to use the platform and get the most out of it. After the pilot, the majority of the salespeople really liked the platform and we moved for purchase. Had I not done this initial call, we wouldn't have gotten buy-in, and, even if we did purchase the tool, it probably would have sat on the metaphorical shelf.

How Do You Get Buy-In to Purchase Marketing Technology?

In a LinkedIn poll of 563 marketers, 39 percent said it was most difficult to get buy-in from the IT department, followed by a close 38 percent who said it was most difficult to get buy-in from executive leadership (Figure 10.1).

How Do You Go About Getting Buy-In from Different Groups?

First, you want to outline the goals and objectives of what the particular Martech tool is going to provide. For example, if you are

FIGURE 10.1 LinkedIn Poll Results

Who is the most difficult to get buy-in for a new Martech tool or Martech strategy?

You can see how people vote. **Learn more**

Executive Leadership	38%
Sales ✓	15%
Marketing	7%
IT (Information Technology)	39%

563 votes • Poll closed • **Remove vote**

purchasing a content experience tool, you should outline the key goals that you're looking to accomplish by implementing the tool. Goals should either be in the form of a revenue-driving activity or time-saving activity—which can also be "productivity gained." From a financial standpoint, we're looking at either increasing revenue or saving/cutting costs.

The goals of a content experience tool are to create an interactive content browsing experience to help improve engagement and generate more leads for the client-business. Such platforms also direct potential customers to relevant content and helps them discover more information about the company and what it can offer them. They also offer an easy way for customers to get in touch with sales if they want to continue the conversation. This enables more opportunities to generate meaningful leads, close deals, and drive revenue. The secondary goal of such platforms, however, is to save marketers' time. They make it easy to host a variety of different content, from blogs to e-books, white papers, videos, podcasts, and audio files—all through the same platform. This can save marketers several hours per week in having to post content in different areas. It can additionally cut down on the amount of effort it takes to direct customers to new content that they may feel is valuable.

Let's take another example. If you're implementing an A/B testing tool, the goals of this application are to increase the conversion rate across your marketing campaigns. If possible, it's a great idea to predict or forecast what kind of improvements you can expect based on either industry data or historical company performance data. For example, if you know that in a similar company, one of your present colleagues implemented such a testing tool and was able to increase conversions by 15 percent, it's reasonable to expect the same sort of results for you. Increased conversions means either more leads came into the funnel, or a higher percentage of leads were converted into deals—in either case leading to more revenue for the business. There's also a secondary goal of being able to run tests easier than without the tool, saving marketers time and money and enabling them to run more experiments. Another way you can obtain buy-in is by performing a gap analysis.

FIGURE 10.2 Customer Touchpoints for Gap Analysis

Gap Analysis

A gap analysis is where you take inventory of the different tools that you have in your tech stack and map them to the different functional goals that you may have. For example, if you're defining your functions as demand generation, customer engagement and sales enablement, you need to look at your tech stack and make sure that you have tools to support each of these (Figure 10.2).

For a more specific example, say your plan is to launch webinars, generate leads, engage those leads with some sort of content experience, and then have sales follow up on those leads that have already been engaged. In this case, there are three key technologies that you need: webinar or online conference software to generate leads; a content experience platform to engage prospects; and a sales automation/cadence tool, so that salespeople can easily follow up on all leads/prospects at scale. With this in mind, you can now answer the question: Do you have the different technologies necessary to support the overall marketing strategy?

Potential ROI Analysis

Another way to gain buy-in—especially from leadership and finance teams—is by conducting a "potential ROI analysis." This demonstrates the expected return on investment for implementing a new Martech tool or strategy.

For example, let's say your salespeople are able to convert 10 percent of leads into an opportunity, and 30 percent of opportunities into a deal. The average deal size is $50,000, which means you are generating $X per salesperson, per quarter. When looking at implementing a new sales automation tool, you can expect the lead-to-opportunity conversion rate to rise to 50 percent. This in turn will increase the number of opportunities, deals closed, and—ultimately—revenue gained. You can then use the ROI calculation formula to determine the potential ROI of a tool by taking the forecasted revenue generated, subtracting the cost of the investment, and diving the result by the cost of the initial investment. In this example, if the tool costs $30,000 per year, the expected return on investment would be Y percent.

An additional way to demonstrate ROI is in the form of costs-saved and time-saved. Let's say, for example, that you want to purchase a new project management tool for marketers. In this scenario, marketers can execute or implement ten campaigns per month, and spend about 40 hours per month creating those campaigns. With the introduction of a project management tool, you can estimate that you're going to cut that time in half. The project management tool may therefore be used to double productivity over the original 40 hours, or save 20 hours executing the same ten campaigns per month. This can equate to salary-hours saved. For example, if marketers are making $120 per hour, and there are five marketers actively building campaigns, then you can save an average of $12,000 per month. This is a great way to demonstrate potential ROI.

Now, I do have to caveat this and point out that, sometimes, the ROI potential is not as clear cut. For example, you may have multiple tools and multiple different strategies at play. This makes it difficult to attribute ROI to one specific initiative. Another thing to keep in mind is that ROI potential is heavily based on forecasts and predictions, which are subject to being wrong and wildly off target.

Also, don't forget the fact that there's opportunity costs for everything that you do. However, this is a great mindset, or frame of reference, on how to think about doing an ROI analysis. Your stakeholders and leadership will greatly appreciate the effort and the thought that goes into trying to make an ROI analysis.

Involving People in the Decision-Making Process

The next thing to do in terms of getting buy-in to purchase more tech tools is to involve people in the decision-making and the tool selection. You do that by setting up meetings and alignments, and even surveys, to try to understand what the stakeholders' key pain points in their sales and marketing efforts are, and what they want to improve. If you can outline a tool that will help them solve their problems, it's much easier to get their buy-in.

Let's say, for example, there are a significant number of leads in your database that are missing key fields. Your conversations with marketers reveal that they are not able to target accounts effectively or personalize campaigns to the extent that they would like. When you talk to the sales team, they share that they don't have the intel on hand to have effective conversations with their prospects. While this may seem obvious to some, you'd be surprised by how many marketing and sales professionals don't know how much their work is improved by data.

After you have done the work to uncover these pain points, you can offer a solution. Your stakeholders will be pleased to hear that a data enrichment service can update and populate missing data, enabling them to launch their customer engagement efforts more effectively. This is a great way to gain consensus and support for the budget and usage of the service.

Involving Stakeholders in the Tool/Vendor Selection

It is helpful to include key stakeholders, especially people who are going to be using it, in the decision in the tool/vendor selection.

For example, if you're going to purchase a new project management tool for marketing, it's a good idea to have all marketers review the features, look at comparison charts, and make a list of "needs to haves" and "nice to haves." The best way to accomplish this with the most insight and the least risk is a trial or pilot period. This enables marketers to try out the software to see if it will meet their needs. One of the worst things that you can do is purchase technology without getting the opinion or buy-in from your stakeholders. It's very common (unfortunately) to see companies rolling out new software applications, only to realize months later that no one likes it, and no one is using it. This can be a big waste of time and money.

Building Effective Relationships

A key topic that often goes overlooked is the value of building effective relationships.

It is important not only to network outside of your organization, but also inside your organization. You need to identify key leaders and influential people within your organization and build strong working relationships with them. This will give you insight about how you can support your co-workers, and keep in touch with the workings of your organization, especially if it's a large enterprise organization.

Keep in mind that relationship building will also occur organically. Each day, we are working with, and collaborating with, others, and building our own reputations by the work we do and the results we deliver. This is one of the best ways to earn trust. However, we should never just sit back and wait for these opportunities to happen. Try to set up open workshops and sessions and invite key stakeholders to talk about what they're working on, what their goals are, and what some of their pain points are, and how you can solve them using Martech. Building those effective working and productive relationships will pay dividends in the future.

Efficiency and Productivity Gains

Now let's talk about efficiency and productivity. Marketing technology can greatly improve the productivity of marketers.

A great example is purchasing an email and landing page self-service tool that enables you to save time. There are applications that you design your own landing pages without the need of a developer or designer. This opens up those resources to focus on other high-value projects, or in the case of outsourcing, you may be able to cut costs altogether. This saves you both time and money. Eliminating the number of resources and dependencies required for each product can help skyrocket your productivity.

Gaining Market Share

One other, often neglected, way to gain buy-in is the idea of overtaking your competition and gaining market share, especially when it comes to audience building. Investing in social media marketing tools, or event platforms, or other pieces of technology, can really drive branding and increase awareness across your target audience and your total addressable market. A strong brand is incredibly valuable. A strong brand ensures you are top of mind for prospects when they are trying to solve a particular problem. This is also known as being part of the "consideration set." Being included in those overarching conversations and being known as one of the top service providers in your category, as well as and building a really strong brand around your niche or target industry, is a motivator for investing in Martech. While you may not be able to quantify revenue potential down to the dollar, the idea of building an audience is one that is easily grasped by leadership and stakeholders.

Long-Term Success

Another thing that you can think about when you're trying to get buy-in for Martech is overall long-term success. When it comes to long-term success, you want to build a marketing strategy that's supported by technology that's going to be repeatable and scalable over time. If your teams are always working to the last minute, giving everything they've got to deliver results, that is not sustainable over time as they will quickly burn out. Martech can help multiply the efforts of your team, which will compound over time and help your company have continuing, upward momentum. Martech can help your team gain leverage for the long-term.

Gaining Momentum

Here's a personal story from my experience about the importance of gaining momentum. I had worked very hard to get buy-in to work with a new data enrichment vendor. I spent time educating and motivating stakeholders to support this new initiative. However, we ended up having some legal contract negotiations, as well as some security concerns over data and personal identifiable information. The key challenge that I had was not getting enough buy-in from top leadership. I also could have thought through some of the implications beforehand, therefore preventing any loss of momentum.

By the time that we had gone through contract negotiations, several months had passed, and many key stakeholders had forgotten that we were launching this initiative, and we had to get approval, buy-in, and budget all over again. It's worth mentioning that you not only have to get buy-in at the beginning, you also have to consistently reinforce the reasons throughout the entire process.

How Do You Get Buy-In for People to Use Martech?

In a Linkedin poll of 685 marketers, 44 percent of marketers said that the number one reason for cancelling a Martech platform contract was lack of adoption. This underscores how important adoption is when considering Martech (Figure 10.3).

Now we'll move into the subject of adoption, which means ensuring that people actively utilize the Martech platform. The first thing you want to be clear about is your purpose and vision for the tool. Stakeholders, for example, marketing and sales people, need to understand why you're using the tool. Is it to generate more leads? Is it to engage customers in a better way? Is it to convert more customers? Is it to nurture customers? Is it to help improve reporting to enable better decisions to be made?

The goals for the purchase of the Martech should highlight the business outcomes and benefits that you want to get from Martech. Most business professionals can relate to, and get behind doing something, if

FIGURE 10.3 Results of a LinkedIn Poll

What is your top reason for cancelling/quitting a Martech platform?

You can see how people vote. **Learn more**

Lack of Adoption	**44%**
Going with a Competitor	**14%**
Lost Budget	**4%**
Lack of ROI ✓	**37%**

685 votes • Poll closed • **Remove vote**

it's going to generate positive business results, because that leads to positive results for everyone, including hiring more people, promotions, and overall business success. Make sure that this purpose for this new Martech tool is documented in some sort of shareable format, such as a Word document that you share with your stakeholders.

Here's an example. Let's say you are implementing a new marketing attribution tool. The purpose of this attribution tool is to understand how each of your marketing campaigns are affecting business results. You are trying to determine which marketing campaigns are the best at driving revenue, and which ones can be improved, with the ultimate objective of improving business results by learning from the high-performing campaigns and improving, or eliminating, the low-performing campaigns. It's vital to ensure everyone knows, and understands, this. It's a good idea to link to your original purpose and vision in all communication about this particular tool.

How to Write a Business Case for Martech

Here is a simple way to write a business case for Martech. Create a document with the following sections: Purpose, Background, Challenges, Recommendations, and Frequently Asked Questions.

Purpose: Be clear about the purpose of your document and what you are asking. For example, your purpose statement could look like: "The purpose of this document is to outline the problems with our data quality and to recommend a data solution to address it."

Background: A background paragraph will give all the contextual information the reader needs to know about the problem. Think about who your reader is for the document, to help you determine what will go into the background. For example, if your document is to be read by marketing practitioners, you can keep the narrative shorter and focus on the details. If your document is going to be read by executives, then you want to start at the beginning.

Challenges: The challenges section is simply that, outlining the problem at hand and the ramifications. Be succinct about what the problem is, why it is happening, and the business impact of the problem. For example, if the problem is that you have poor data quality, convey that sales and marketing people are unable to use the data for customer engagements, and that reports shared with the larger company are inaccurate, which can greatly skew decision-making.

Recommendation: The recommendation section is where you outline the solution, which will include the Martech tool you propose. Write down what the solution is and how exactly it will solve the problem. It's also a good idea to show that you considered other options and why you ended up choosing this one as your primary recommendation. The recommendation should also explain what the next steps are, and actions that need to be taken by the reader.

Frequently Asked Questions: The frequently asked questions section is where you cover information that the reader would like to know, but is not included in the above sections because that would have made it confusing. Remember that you don't want to overwhelm your reader with technical details at first, but you also don't want to hide anything or leave anything out. This is why it is important to have a frequently asked questions section.

Training and Enablement

Training is an important part of the Martech strategy that is often overlooked. Training is important, because if your team does not know how to use a specific marketing application, the chances are that they won't use it. Training should come in different forms. You should offer live, in-person training, virtual training, checklists, recorded webinars, and more. My preferred method of training others on the use of Martech is produce official training documentation, as well as roll out each of the aforementioned formats. It's important to realize that people learn in different ways. Some of your team may learn better with a hands-on, practical approach to learning. Others may internalize the material best by reading, or by watching a demo. Make sure to craft clear and concise training materials, including resources where they can learn more.

One example from my career is when I managed the training program to teach hundreds of marketers how to leverage marketing automation. I included live training classes where people attended live, watched demonstrations, and could ask questions. I also created a library of training videos that people could access on demand from wherever they were in the world. My team and I also created playbooks, which are visual checklists that teach marketers how to use marketing automation, with a series of instructions as well as screenshots.

I also hosted monthly webinars to share advanced topics so people could attend and learn more and discuss other things that they want to learn. Having all these different training modalities and mediums available gives people the best chance of understanding how to use the tools so they can feel empowered to do their jobs.

Change Management

Change management is incredibly important, because whenever you implement something new, it requires a change of process or a change in the way people do things. For example, implementing a new sales automation tool may entail sellers having to change from using their personal work email accounts to using a different platform, with different features and functionality. Even transitioning to using different internal products and platforms requires change management. It's a very human characteristic to be resistant to change, and it typically stems from the fear of the unknown, or a reluctance to take on additional work. People tend to get really secure and in a comfort zone when it comes to habits in the way that they work.

Here are some tips to making sure that you're rolling out change in the right way. First, communicate the vision. We talked about this earlier, but people need to understand the reasoning and improved business outcomes behind implementing a new Martech tool, or a new way to use Martech. The next key is to clearly communicate what is to be expected. For example, when rolling out a new Martech platform, ensure people know that the change is happening, when they can attend training sessions, and how they can get started. In addition, it's a good idea to mention how the success of an initiative will be measured.

When you are managing any type of change, remember that if you are not over-communicating, it is likely that you are not communicating enough. Not only should you announce a change or new Martech tool, but you should also send several different reminders in as many different channels as possible. Remind people over Slack or instant message, send out email newsletters, hold open forums, and in your company's general announcements.

Here is my method when it comes to large scale change management initiatives. The first thing that I like to do is set up a working session about the intent to do the change and invite key stakeholders before any official decision has been made. This way people understand the purpose ahead of time and are also involved in the decision-making. This gives them the opportunity to point out potential flaws about the new application or process, as well as unaddressed needs. The great thing about these pre-meetings is that I usually learn something extra that I couldn't have by doing siloed research. After this initial session, I'll make sure to amend the plan based on any key changes, and then share the announcements of the official plan. Finally, I will make sure my plan is over-communicated. I'll send emails, notices in instant message groups, and announce the plan in marketing meetings to drive the message home.

After the initial announcement, I'll also follow up and thank the key stakeholders for participating and let them know what the result of the meeting was. Then I'll create a timeline, so that all stakeholders know when to expect the change and the different things that they need to do leading up to the change over the course of the next few weeks. I provide them with ample time to prepare for the change. I'll send multiple reminders, and also call out key people that I want to make sure are on board. After the change has been implemented, I will monitor it from a technology standpoint, both to see if the change is being followed, and to work with any people that need additional help to actually see through the change. Then, a few weeks after this, I report on how what the status of the change was and if it was successful or not. This may seem like a lot of messages and a lot of work, but believe me, especially an enterprise organization, the way you manage change can be the difference between success and failure.

How Do You Measure Buy-In for Martech?

There's three key ways to measure buy-in for Martech tool or strategy: adoption, return on investment, and stakeholder sentiment. The first one is adoption. I like to measure adoption in the terms of green, yellow, and red. Green means we're getting almost full adoption across the board. So, let's say we have our new testing tool, if 90 percent of marketers are using the testing tool on a regular basis, I would categorize that as green. Yellow means average adoption, which means there is room for improvement.

Here is an example of when adoption could be marked yellow. If 50 percent of marketers are using the testing tool on a semi-regular basis, this means that there is room for significant improvement.

Red is minimal adoption. Adoption would be marked red if, in our testing example, we had very few or only a handful of marketers using the testing tool, and the majority of marketers were not using the tool, because they don't know about it, they don't know what to use it for, or they don't see the value in it.

Measuring adoption by color categorization and then creating plans for each color will help greatly reduce under-utilization. If, for some reason, these efforts are unsuccessful, it might be time to look at deeper causes.

It's critical to push yourself to try and measure the return on investment for every single tool. If the tool leads to revenue, it's a little bit easier because you can frame the return on investment in terms of an increase in number of leads generated, opportunities converted, or revenue generated. At times, you may have to measure Martech ROI by efficiency and productivity. This is done by reporting on how many hours are saved, or how many additional projects you were able to complete because of the tool. Finally, you always want to measure stakeholder sentiment. Stakeholder sentiment means what feedback do stakeholders, or users of the tool, have regarding this application. Do they like it? Do they feel like it serves their needs? Are they getting a return from it? How would they rate it on a scale of one to five? Use stakeholder surveys (you can use free survey tools like Google Forms or low-cost tools like Survey Monkey) to survey all your stakeholders and get a good sense of the tools working out for them or not.

Here are some sample questions:

- On a scale of one to five, how would you rate this application?
- How often do you use this tool?
- On a scale of one to five, how would you rate the effectiveness of this tool?
- On a scale of one to five, how would you rate your knowledge and proficiency of using this tool?
- On a scale of one to five, do you feel that we're getting return on investment from this tool?

Finally, you always want to have an open-ended question to see if you can capture additional thoughts from the survey-taker.

Setting Expectations

One of the worst things you can do when driving a Martech strategy throughout an organization is to set wrong expectations. Imagine if your stakeholders get excited, and truly believe a new platform will solve all their work problems. It will be an uncomfortable conversation once they find this not to be true. Make sure you are not over-promising and under-delivering. Your stakeholders need to understand that any forecasted results are going to be intelligent predictions based on historical data. You need to explain that it will be learning process. We always have to remember that the best laid plans can fail sometimes, and that setting the proper expectations can help you earn trust long-term.

Summary

- Buy-in is key for Martech because people and stakeholders are the ones that use it.
- Use ROI analysis and projections to win stakeholders over to Martech.
- The key to buy-in is alignment and internal communication.
- You can measure buy-in through adoption and user sentiment.

11

Continual Improvement and the Future of Martech

When we talk about continual improvement in Martech, we are referring to the continual measurement, evaluation, and optimization of your marketing technology stack to see if it is helping you achieve your marketing objectives. As any good business knows, it's always important to continually set new goals for higher sales for more revenue to gain more customers. You're constantly going to be moving the goalposts, therefore, you should be constantly evolving your Martech strategy. That's also important because with the advancements of technology and the dynamic marketplace, your team is going to need to be very agile.

Why is Continual Improvement Important?

I've always believed in the philosophy that a business is either getting better, or it's getting worse. This means that there really isn't such a thing as a business plateau. The same can be said for your tech stack and Martech strategy, and all of the systems and processes you put in place to support Martech. Your Martech performance is either getting better or worse. How do you know if it's getting worse? Your systems are slowing down and your data is becoming stale. In short—you are starting to move away from the path to your business goals.

The key thing to think about when it comes to controlling continual improvement is long-term business impact. When you invest in the practice of continually reviewing your marketing technology and continually asking the question, "Are we performing the way that we should be?," this has the effect of continually making your overall tech stack, marketing, and business in general better over time.

One of the important things to consider that goes beyond Martech is really creating a culture of continual improvement and continual learning with a desire to always improve.

For example, in recent years, Satya Nadella, the CEO of Microsoft, changed the mantra at Microsoft from "know it all culture" to "learn it all culture." (Microsoft.com) This simple change illustrates the mindset of growth. Similarly, one of Amazon's leadership principles is to "learn and be curious." Leaders must grasp the fact that they will never know everything. We should instead be curious about how things work and how things can be improved for the customer.

Make sure to continually think of how you can improve your marketing and your technology for the best possible customer experience.

How Do You Make Sure Your Martech Strategy is Continually Improving?

In a recent LinkedIn poll of 403 marketers, 44 percent said that the way they continue to make sure their Martech stack improves is to "talk to peers and colleagues." The next most popular response was to do self-audits and self-research (32 percent) (Figure 11.1).

While these are important components of a long-term growth strategy for Martech, it's important to look at it from multiple dimensions.

Let's unpack how we actually create continual improvement in Martech. First, every year create a three-year vision and three-year roadmap of what the future of your tech stack looks like. Some will even benefit from looking at longer horizons, such as five or ten years. The key here is that you are thinking far into the future, and thinking big about what you want your overall marketing strategy to look

FIGURE 11.1   Results of LinkedIn Poll

What is your preferred way to evaluate your Martech stack and Martech strategy to make sure you continue to improve long term?

You can see how people vote. **Learn more**

Attend/learn from conferences	12%
Consultant/agency consultation	12%
Talk to peers and colleauges	44%
Self research and self audit ✓	32%

403 votes · Poll closed · **Remove vote**

like. This way, you're never really tempted to fall into degression with your Martech—you are always referring to a plan to improve.

You can do this by asking a few questions:

1 What kind of ROI are we expecting from our Martech stack and strategy?

2 In three years, what kind of tools and platforms will we have in place?

3 How will our marketers and salespeople interact with the tools and the data in three years?

4 How are we creating a technology stack that will support our customers in three years?

5 How can we make sure that our data (and our customers' data) is secure in three years?

Every year, make sure that you have a clear vision of what you want your business to look like in the future.

The next point is to constantly evaluate if you're meeting performance expectations. This is very similar to marketing and business in general, where you're taking a look at a certain time period, setting goals and consistently asking yourself if you're achieving those goals. For example, if you have a lead or revenue number that you're supposed to hit each quarter, and you're missing it by 10–20 percent, then you are not hitting your goals. This gives you the opportunity to think about your marketing and marketing strategy, and ask if there are ways that you can adjust the way your technology works. Perhaps there is a new tool or a new strategy that might enable you to hit these goals? For example, let's say that you're not able to convert enough leads on your website because you have limited salespeople and marketing campaigns. You could think about implementing a conversational marketing tool like a chatbot that can answer common questions and prompt website visitors to submit their information, talk to a salesperson, or schedule a demo with a salesperson. Thinking this way allows you to continually reflect on the tools and tech you need to help achieve your goals.

Leverage Strategy and Product Frameworks

To continue making sure you improve your Martech strategy in the long-term, use frameworks that help improve the business strategy and the customer experience. We've talked already about how operating Martech can be made better by treating your entire tech stack like a product. Here are some frameworks that business and product leaders use, adapted for Martech.

Spotify: Think It, Build It, Ship It, Tweak It

The first is a product framework adapted from Spotify, originally developed for product managers (Bank, 2014). The framework is: think it, build it, ship it, tweak it.

Think it: In this stage, you are identifying a problem you want to solve with marketing technology, researching and brainstorming to come up with ways to solve it. This could be a simple internet search or meeting with a group of peers to dissect the problem. Once you have a shortlist of viable solutions, use the prioritization frameworks described in earlier chapters to decide upon a solution worth testing.

Build it: For Martech, this refers to running a pilot program to test if the feature or tool that you are rolling out will effectively solve your problem. For example, if you believe a direct mail platform will help your opportunity conversion rate improve, this is the phase where you would run a limited pilot. Be clear about success metrics for your pilot, and what level of success would be enough to move forward with a full contract.

Ship it: Once you have ideally tested multiple solutions, prepare and execute a rollout plan to ensure adoption and success. Remember that users need to know why a tool is being deployed, how to use it, and what actions they should take next. Creating and following through with an adoption plan puts you on the best path for success.

Tweak it: Regularly review your new product or feature in terms of intended output as well as user feedback.

Amazon: PRFAQ

The book *Working Backwards* (Bryar and Carr, 2021) documents the Press Release Frequently Asked Questions (PRFAQ) framework popularized by Amazon. It can be used by business and product leaders right before the launch of a new initiative. The idea is that you write a press release about a new initiative in a future state, to be read by customers. Why is this beneficial? Because it helps you look ahead and think about what customers really care about, and what impact you want the initiative to have on them. Now, it doesn't always have to be about external customers. The PRFAQ is just an exercise after all, and you can apply the same to your internal stakeholders. The key here is that you are really going after the "why" of your projects and initiatives—rather than doing them for the sake of it. Too many teams will implement tools or features just because it is possible, not because of the business outcomes it will produce. The FAQ-aspect of the PRFAQ clarifies what is actually happening and takes the reader through your idea. This also forces you to think through the project by putting yourself in your customers' shoes and asking what people outside of the organization would really think. The exercise of listing out these questions-and-answers may also reveal some blind spots that you haven't thought about.

PRFAQ IN ACTION: SENDOSO

Headline: ABC Company chooses Sendoso to Improve Customer Engagement and Retention

New York City, NY January 1, 2022.

International services firm ABC Company announces the launch of their partnership with Sendoso, a direct mail platform, to improve the engagement with their customers and increase their retention rate. Before today, ABC Company had few methods of engaging with their customer base outside of virtual meetings and conferences. Using the Sendoso direct mail platform, ABC Company is able to engage both small and large customers with personalized gifts via mail. These gifts can either be Sendoso-branded swag items such as t-shirts, sweaters, and coffee mugs, in addition to personalized gift cards to the customer's favorite retailer. "I'm impressed with the appreciation that ABC Company is showing their customers!" states John Smith, Vice President of Financial Services at XYZ Inc. "After our quarterly business review, the team and I received personalized gift cards to our favorite restaurants. We will never forget ABC Company's care for their customers, that's for sure!"

After 3 months of implementing Sendoso's direct mail engagement platform, ABC Company saw a 30% increase in customer satisfaction, and anticipates over 1 million dollars in saved revenue via renewals. The success of this three-month pilot will be followed by a full investment to launch direct mail across North America and Europe, with the rest of the world regions shortly after.

FAQs

Why are we launching Sendoso?

We are launching Sendoso's direct mail platform in order to improve customer engagement and retention, and to overall show our appreciation to our customers. While other methods of engagement have had modest success, direct mail is a great, tangible way to get in front of customers and make a memorable impact.

What are we doing to do with it?

Sendoso's direct mail platform allows us to automatically send personalized gifts to customers based on a triggering event. For example, after large meetings such as a quarterly business review (QBR), we can send personalized gift cards to all members of the customer's team that attended. In addition, we can also send thank you and appreciation gifts (such as Sendoso-branded swag) ahead of renewal dates so that we can stay top of mind with customers during this critical time period. The personalized gifts are going to be tailored to each customer based on their interests (recorded by account manager) and local favorites based on their city.

How are we going to send the personalized gifts?

Sendoso integrates directly with our CRM, Salesforce.com, and can trigger direct mail gifts off of the events that we configure. For example, once we log a meeting in Salesforce, we can have Sendoso automatically send gifts the following week. The integration with Sendoso is in real-time, and can be triggered with or without human approval.

How will we know if this is working?

We are measuring the success of Sendoso through our monthly customer surveys, number of customer touchpoints, positive feedback from customers, and renewal rates.

The above PRFAQ demonstrates how the writer is thinking about the business impact to launching this direct mail platform, as well as thoughtfully considering the questions that may arise from the team.

Invest in Marketing Operations

The next aspect of continual improvement focuses on investment in marketing operations to develop its role in the organizational structure. A marketing operations team operates your company's tech stack, and focuses on the tools, processes, and metrics that help execute great marketing.

By investing in a good marketing operations leader and team, you are making sure that you have the talent in place to run your Martech stack effectively and continually identify growth opportunities. There a few things that you want to think about when building out your Martech marketing operations team.

First, the talent on the team needs to have a strong balance between business acumen and technical expertise. They don't necessarily need to be developers, but they should understand the technical element of marketing, and should be skilled and versed in marketing automation, databases reporting, analytics, and most areas of digital and B2B marketing.

Second, you want to make sure that you have people to cover the different functional areas of marketing operations. One of my favorite ways to break this down is to have dedicated marketing operations for the following areas: marketing engineering, which builds internal products and processes for marketing; reporting and analytics, which supports regular marketing reports and insights; system administration, which manages and governs the different platforms of your tech stack; and training and enablement, which supports stakeholders as they adopt and utilize Martech.

These different core areas should have specialists that run them like a business, continually improving the overall use of your marketing technology.

THE RISE OF MARKETING OPERATIONS

Marketing operations is one of marketing's fastest growing functions, and it is common to see companies struggling to hire great marketing operations talent. What once was a role that was the last hire on the marketing team is quickly becoming one of the most important functions that a marketing leader hires for. There are a number of reasons for both this recent emphasis on—as well as growth of—the role:

- proximity to data;
- exposure to multiple areas of the business;
- focus on execution.

Proximity to data: As marketing becomes increasingly data-driven, the marketers that work with data regularly are the ones that will develop the skills to really make an impact. In addition, organizations need marketers who are able to read data and pull insights from the noise. Marketing operations professionals work with data day-in and day-out, ensuring information gets transferred from digital customer touchpoints all the way to data visualization tools. The marketing operations team is also often responsible for creating and delivering the critical business reports and dashboards that executives use to make overarching business decisions.

Exposure to multiple areas of the business: Marketing operations professionals are also in-demand because they excel at working cross-functionally with many different teams. A typical day in marketing operations would have them working with sales, product, marketing, finance, customer success, and other teams in order to complete their projects. Since the emphasis on technology brings many groups together, businesses need talent that excels in an increasingly collaborative environment.

Focus on execution: The growth of marketing operations is also due to the role's extreme focus on execution. Marketing operations professionals are the ones that take strategy and turn it into reality. This is accomplished by taking marketing plans and creating assets, managing data, targeting audiences, deploying campaigns, and reporting on results. While many marketers may spend all of their time on thinking about strategy, marketing operations thrives in trying new tactics, getting real feedback from the customers, and making quick pivots to drive the best results.

Conducting Martech Stack Audits

The next thing to consider when trying to continually improve your Martech strategy is conducting self-audits. A great way to conduct a self-audit is to run a gap analysis on your current tech stack. You can also seek feedback from stakeholders and have monthly workshops to identify key pain points and ways to address their needs. These stakeholders should include top-level leadership and team leaders to understand where the improvement areas are, and if there is any way technology can support those improvements. If there's any problems in those areas, then it might require changing your strategy.

The next closely related topic is working with an agency or consultant to do a third-party audit. A third-party audit (or an agency audit) benefits you from an objective, fresh set of eyes and experience to review your marketing technology stack. An agency likely works with many different businesses across different industries and sizes, and can bring broad expertise to your technology stack, recommending key integrations, key tools that you should be using, and also how to set up and configure your tools/platforms to get the most out of your Martech strategy.

Similarly, in order to continually improve you should be running small experiments and pilots whenever possible. This really comes down to being agile and practicing the principles of agile marketing, which essentially means to work in sprints and receive constant feedback. It's important to continually run small experiments because they allows you to test new things that you may or may not know to work—and to get feedback very quickly.

One way to ensure a culture of experimentation is to have regularly scheduled A/B tests. Run these experiments across your website, email channels and social media channels to figure out what works best and what customers respond to the most. You can also run other experiments such as advertising on different channels using other platforms. When it comes to testing new platforms, try assigning a group of power users or marketers who are tech savvy, and see what kind of results they are getting.

For example, my team and I identified a group of sophisticated email marketers and identified them as good candidates to run a pilot for email merchandising—creating dynamic, real-time crafted emails that may have been too technical for the average marketer. We wanted to see if email merchandising could improve the customer experience, and since this pilot we've seen great engagement rates—giving us a strong good foundation for doing something larger around email merchandising.

CONTINUAL IMPROVEMENT AND THE FUTURE OF MARTECH   225

I do want to mention one thing about running small pilots and small experiments: it's important to know how to run experiments correctly. You have to run business experiments the way that you would run a scientific experiment. First, you should split your audience into two groups—a test group and a control group. The test group is going to be exposed to the initiative, while the control group will remain not receive any exposure to the initiative.

Both groups also need to be homogenous. Random sampling can help to ensure this, but you still have to check manually just in case. You should also check the statistical significance of your experiments to make sure that you're working with a large enough sample size. You can do this by using some simple statistical significance calculators online to see how confident you are about the results.

Always make sure you're running experiments the correct way. Otherwise, the results of your experiments may be flawed.

Industry Learning and Research

The next part of continual improvement that I want to emphasize is continually learning about the industry and the technology available—as well as continually improving your skills.

A great way to do this this is to attend Martech and marketing conferences, and there are a diverse set available today. This gives you the opportunity to learn from thought leaders, different groups, and see the different vendors all in one place. It also gives you great opportunity to meet and network with like-minded professionals.

Another great way to continue learning is to read/purchase analyst reports. Firms like Gartner and Forrester—and even Martech-specific organizations like Martech.org and Chief Martech—provide a wealth of information on the industry. They often conduct surveys and other forms of industry research to see how marketing technology is growing and the impact Martech is having on the overall business landscape. Analyst reports can give you a great idea of where you should benchmark your organization and if you are lacking in specific areas.

My personal favorite way to learn is to talk to peers and join a community of Martech professionals. In my career, one of the best ways that I've learned how to solve marketing technology problems is to is to connect with experts who are doing it already. Presently, many tech vendors support different groups, as well as different user groups. You can attend those meetings, learn about new topics, and meet your peers. It's always great to have a sounding board, to brainstorm with your peers, or even connect with people more senior to you about the issues that you're addressing with Martech. Collectively, they can sometimes provide out-of-the-box ideas that can help you.

If possible, you should join a community. These communities can be in-person, or online communities, such as forums, social media networking groups, and Slack communities.

Another of my favorites is to take formal courses, read books (like this one!), and listen to podcasts about Martech. There is a plethora of different resources out there that you can learn from about the different areas of Martech and ways to improve your skills.

Study Project Management and Program Management

This might surprise you, but continuing to learn and develop your skills in project management and program management can directly improve your work in Martech. That's because the implementation or execution of marketing can actually be broken up into projects, so the nature of work is highly project-based. But even more so, when you treat work like a project, it helps you keep your goals and outcomes in mind, scope your resources and budget correctly, and will help you identify bottlenecks. When you look at your work through this lens, you can better come up with ways where marketing technology can help you achieve your goals. Here are things you should consider when looking to improve your project and program management skills.

Study the Project Management Professional (PMP) certification materials: This doesn't necessarily mean that you need to pass the exam and become certified. However, I highly recommend going through the books and online programs as they will give you a strong foundation in how to manage a project and what to watch out for. One of the key things that help in Martech—especially with migrations, product implementations, and pilots—is to create an estimated timeline of how long everything will take. It may be tempting to just work off of a checklist and move on to the next item when the first is completed. However, do not do this. There is incredible value to planning and resource management to coming up with a timeline (even if it is a guess) because it creates deadlines and helps you look around the corner for potential problems.

Study agile project management and agile marketing: Agile project management is a method of project management that encourages frequent delivery of work and frequent feedback by end-users and customers. This is a departure from the traditional method, sometimes called the "waterfall method" of project management where everything is planned to the last detail beforehand, and then work is meticulously planned out, which can lead to problems if there is any variance or changes to the plan. Check out *The Six Disciplines of Agile Marketing* by Jim Ewel or *The Agile Marketer* by Roland Smart to gain an understanding of the fundamentals of agile project management for marketers. One of the key things to learn from agile best practices is the concept of the standup meeting, which is a brief, daily meeting to coordinate everyone on the team. One of the best versions of the standup meeting is to have each member state their goals for the day and if there is anything that is preventing them from reaching those goals. This way, other team members can offer to help, or offer solutions that might unblock problems. You can also use this meeting to cover a quick list of issues that have come up in the past day, and the next action items to solve them. Be careful not to try to solve the issues in the meeting itself unless the problem can be solved in under two minutes. Remember that the purpose of this meeting is coordination and collaboration, rather than to solve specific issues.

The Future of Martech

Here are things you want to watch out for in the future marketing technology:

Martech Talent and Remote Work

The COVID-19 pandemic creating a new culture of remote work, and the landscape for experienced Martech professionals in becoming scarce. Never forget that an effective Martech strategy always takes talent and time to come to fruition. Larger companies should invest heavily in building out their Martech teams and planning ahead to dedicate sufficient headcount to managing Martech technology and marketing processes. Smaller companies with less resources should start training their staff early on the value of Martech, as well as enroll their employees in courses to level-up their digital marketing and Martech skills.

Martech Consolidation

Another thing to watch out for is the continued consolidation of the Martech space. Because there are large Martech service providers with incredible financial resources, it is common for vendors to acquire other similar or complementary platforms. While it is difficult to plan ahead for these types of changes, it is important to ensure that you are managing your Martech stack effectively like a business. First, ensure you are mitigating risk with each of your Martech platforms. If you have a tool that you are depending on to drive critical business results, make sure you have a backup plan if that tool is no longer available. Remember to always think 3–5 years ahead in terms of business need and the overall economic landscape. You also want to think about where you are getting your data from. If you depend heavily on data vendors in your sales and marketing processes, it is a good idea to have backup vendors or some thoughts on what to do if that data vendor can no longer supply you with the data you need.

The Long-Lasting Martech Platforms Will Focus on Business Impact and Customer Experience

While it may be confusing now because there are so many Martech tools and platforms to choose from, the truth is that the vendors who will win are the ones that focus on business impact and customer experience. While many tools exist and many more will be created to help with minor business tasks, the ones that ultimately generate value for both brands and vendors will be the one that focus on business impact and customer experience. So, whenever you are evaluating tools and comparing vendors, or using a matrix to figure out which tools you need, keep this concept in mind.

Improving the Customer Experience

Finally, one of the key ways to not only continually improve your Martech strategy, but to continually improve your business in general, is to always be thinking about improving the customer experience. Think about your end customer. How are they learning about your company? How are they trying to read the content across your website? How are they finding you and trying to solve their problem?

Continue asking these questions even after acquiring prospects as customers: How are they using your products and services? How are they continually getting more and more return on their investment with you? Are they having a great experience and are they are sharing and telling others? Now, when we look at business through that lens, we're looking at both technical and non-technical ways to support them and create a good customer experience. We can use technology to do that.

Remember that Martech should always be about improving the customer experience.

Summary

- Invest in the continual improvement of Martech because the landscape is always changing.

- You can leverage strategic and product management frameworks to improve Martech.

- Regularly auditing your Martech stack and studying Martech trends can keep you ahead of change.

- The future of Martech will depend highly on the remote workforce, the consolidation of Martech vendors, and the expectations of customers.

REFERENCES

Bank, C. (2014) Building Minimum Viable Products at Spotify [Online] https://speckyboy.com/building-minimum-viable-products-spotify (archived at https://perma.cc/3U3W-LQR5) [accessed 13 June 2022]

Bryar, C. and Carr, B. (2021) *Working Backwards: Insights, stories, and secrets from inside Amazon*, London, Macmillan

Collins, K. (2019) Martech industry 2020: new report on budget, investment, skills, *ClickZ* [Online] www.clickz.com/martech-industry-2020-report/ (archived at https://perma.cc/MT89-VRYC) [accessed 13 June 2022]

Contentmarketinginstitute.com – What is content marketing? [Online] https://contentmarketinginstitute.com/what-is-content-marketing (archived at https://perma.cc/QEJ4-JBUL) [accessed 13 June 2022]

Covey, S. (2007) *The 7 Habits of Highly Effective People*, London, Simon & Schuster

Customer Data Platform Institute – What is a CDP? [Online] www.cdpinstitute.org/learning-center/what-is-a-cdp (archived at https://perma.cc/M7CU-XGRK) [accessed 13 June 2022]

Ewel, J. (2020) *The Six Disciplines of Agile Marketing: Proven practices for more effective marketing and better business results*, Hoboken, NJ, John Wiley & Sons

Finances Online (2021) 72 vital digital transformation statistics: 2021/2022 spending, adoption, analysis & data [Online] https://financesonline.com/digital-transformation-statistics (archived at https://perma.cc/Y3ML-6QAB) [accessed 13 June 2022]

Gartner.com – Integration Platform as a Service (iPaaS) [Online] www.gartner.com/en/information-technology/glossary/information-platform-as-a-service-ipaas (archived at https://perma.cc/H3H8-D635) [accessed 13 June 2022]

Ikajo.com – What is Platform Integration? [Online] https://ikajo.com/glossary/platform-integration (archived at https://perma.cc/2E8F-C37D) [accessed 13 June 2022]

Kitani, K. (2019) The $900 billion reason GE, Ford and P&G failed at digital transformation, *CNBC Evolve* [Online] www.cnbc.com/2019/10/30/heres-why-ge-fords-digital-transformation-programs-failed-last-year.html#:~:text=GE%2C%20Ford%20and%20other%20major,and%20outlook%20with%20their%20employees (archived at https://perma.cc/2BR5-K8JP) [accessed 13 June 2022]

Mailchimp.com – Marketing analytics [Online] https://mailchimp.com/marketing-glossary/marketing-analytics (archived at https://perma.cc/VY92-T8YU) [accessed 13 June 2022]

Microsoft.com – How to introduce a learn-it-all culture in your business: 3 steps to success [Online] https://cloudblogs.microsoft.com/industry-blog/en-gb/cross-industry/2019/10/01/introduce-learn-it-all-culture (archived at https://perma.cc/6SVF-MTV2) [accessed 13 June 2022]

OpenExo (2019) Global transformation ecosystem OpenExO announces ExO World Digital Summit [Online] www.prnewswire.com/news-releases/global-transformation-ecosystem-openexo-announces-exo-world-digital-summit-301029156.html (archived at https://perma.cc/L9LK-6UZL) [accessed 13 June 2022]

Optimizely (2019) What is account-based marketing (ABM)? [Online] www.optimizely.com/optimization-glossary/account-based-marketing (archived at https://perma.cc/J3DE-9JPB) [accessed 13 June 2022]

Productplan.com – What is Technical Debt? [Online] www.productplan.com/glossary/technical-debt (archived at https://perma.cc/WY72-2KA9) [accessed 13 June 2022]

Salesforce.com (2015) What is CRM? [Online] www.salesforce.com/crm/what-is-crm (archived at https://perma.cc/633D-XXP4) [accessed 13 June 2022]

Salesforce.com – What is digital transformation? [Online] www.salesforce.com/products/platform/what-is-digital-transformation (archived at https://perma.cc/3TZK-GYME) [accessed 13 June 2022]

Schwager, A. and Meyer, C. (2007) Understanding customer experience, *Harvard Business Review* [Online] https://hbr.org/2007/02/understanding-customer-experience (archived at https://perma.cc/G45T-GWQB) [accessed 13 June 2022]

Sitecore.com – What is a CMS (Content Management System)? [Online] www.sitecore.com/knowledge-center/digital-marketing-resources/what-is-a-cms (archived at https://perma.cc/3GH5-YBAB) [accessed 13 June 2022]

Smart, R. (2016) *The Agile Marketer: turning customer experience into your competitive advantage*, Hoboken, NJ, John Wiley & Sons

Techtarget.com – CRM (customer relationship management) [Online] www.techtarget.com/searchcustomerexperience/definition/CRM-customer-relationship-management (archived at https://perma.cc/9QXH-NSBE) [accessed 13 June 2022]

Zenithmedia.com – Digital advertising to exceed 60% of global ad spend in 2022 [Online] www.zenithmedia.com/digital-advertising-to-exceed-60-of-global-adspend-in-2022 (archived at https://perma.cc/8GD2-5TZ7) [accessed 13 June 2022]

INDEX

Note: Page numbers in *italics* refer to figures